The Great Arkansas Pie Book

The Great Arkansas Pie Book

Kat Robinson

TONTI PRESS

Published by Tonti Press
Little Rock, Arkansas
Copyright © 2023 by Kat Robinson. All rights reserved.

First published May 2023
Second printing June 2023
Manufactured in the United States of America

ISBN: 978-1-952547-14-0

Library of Congress Control Number: 2023936052

Paperback release September 2023

ISBN: 978-1-952547-13-3

EPUB release September 2023

ISBN: 978-1-952547-12-6

Notice: The information in this book is true and complete to the best of our knowledge. It is offered without guarantee on the part of the author. The author disclaims all liability in connection with the use of this book.

All rights reserved. No part of this book may be reproduced or transmitted in any form whatsoever without prior written permission from the author or publisher, except in the case of brief quotations embodied in critical articles and reviews.

The author accepted no compensation for inclusion of any element in this book. All photographs of food consist of edible, real food not enhanced with photographic tricks, manipulation or fakery.

Photographs for this book were taken primarily by the author, with additional photography provided by Grav Weldon.
Photos provided by the contributors of these recipes are also included where applicable.

To Mary Twedt,
Phyllis Speer and John Philpot.

Y'all cooked so I could dine.

TABLE OF CONTENTS	6
FOREWORD BY CINDY GRISHAM	8
INTRODUCTION	12
CRUSTS	17
FRUIT PIES	27
NUT PIES	63
CREAM PIES	85
CUSTARD AND CHESS PIES	123
CHOCOLATE PIES	169
MERINGUE PIES	191
FRIED PIES AND HAND PIES	211
PIES THAT MAKE THEIR OWN CRUST	219
SAVORY PIES	229
UNIQUE AND UNUSUAL PIES	263
INDEX	277
ABOUT THE AUTHOR	284

FOREWORD

Food historian and critic John T. Edge once wrote that Arkansas is the "most pie mad state" in the South and maybe the nation, and he is not wrong. While many folks think of pie as something that you need the freshest berries or the ripest apples to create, folks in Arkansas have long had to make do with what they had to feed the family, with nary a berry or apple insight. Arkansans have created pie fillings out of things like vinegar when there was nothing left in the cupboard, but… well, vinegar. While things have certainly changed on the financial front in the state over the years, those tried-and-true recipes created by mothers and grandmothers trying to feed a hungry family have become old favorites.

Over the years Arkansans, like folks across the country, realized that it was easier to buy a frozen pie at the store, or pick up a fried pie at the drive through and pie making sort of became a lost art. Then 2020 rolled around and the COVID pandemic hit and pulled a couple of generations of Arkansans back home and into the kitchen. With fast food joints, cafes and restaurants either shut down or just doing take out of a very slim menu, the family suddenly had to find a way to feed the crew on something that did not come from a bag or a box.

There amid the pandemic mess was Kat Robinson. A dedicated foodie, Kat and her ever faithful photographer, food taster and life partner, Grav Weldon; were stuck at home as well, unable to travel and work on another of their stellar books or television specials on Arkansas food. Left to her own devices, much like the rest of the state's residents, she wandered into the kitchen and started pulling out old family recipes and began the process of becoming a baker.

She realized fairly quickly that baking is a sort of weird cross between art and science. If a recipe says to use 1 cup plus

Foreword

1 teaspoon of an ingredient you better do it, or the results are not always pretty, or edible. Don't try changing up the lard for an equal amount of butter or vegetable shortening either. With a bit of practice under her belt though, she began turning out her own brand of delicious, and became determined to show everyone that they too can create yummy greatness.

So, she began corresponding with restaurant owners and their staff on business and community favorites. While I am sure many were hesitant to share their pride and joy, it is not uncommon to have directions and lists of ingredients for baked goods that are kept under lock and key away from even their own family, Kat managed to wrangle up a good-sized pile of recipes to try at home. Along the way, she worked on crafting the perfect pie crust. While that sounds easy it is not, because there is no such thing as the one and only, single, perfect crust for any kind of pie. The result of all her hard work is this book.

Now the photos are not always gorgeous, because sometimes the prettiest pie is not the tastiest pie. Plus, baking is like I said, a cross between art and science. I have been told that my own great grandmother used to say that if a cake didn't fall apart, it wasn't worth eating. It might not be pretty but what it lacked in appearance it made up for in taste. No matter what the outcome though, what a treasure trove of deliciousness Kat has uncovered. From instructions for the best crust of its kind, to pages of recipes about fruit pies, meat pies, veggie pies, and what I can only describe as goo pies because the filling is some sort of concocted goo from chocolate to coconut to vinegar (really, vinegar) to weird combinations of all three. They are all amazingly delicious though and I promise you will enjoy the tales that surround them even if you never venture to attempt the creation yourself.

So, sit back, grab yourself something to drink, and enjoy the contents of this book. You will be glad you did.

Cindy Grisham
Author, **A Savory History of Arkansas Delta Food: Potlikker, Coon Suppers & Chocolate Gravy**

A special thanks goes to The Writers' Colony at Dairy Hollow, where recipes for this book were tested, photographed and tasted.

More thanks goes to all the contributors, cookbook assembly teams, church groups, community organizations, food writers, home cooks, restaurant chefs, culinary students, researchers, authors, and family members who have taken time over the decades to write down these pie recipes and keep them for future generations to enjoy.

And to my readers:
Your support over the years has been extraordinary. I am thankful for every encouraging word, suggestion, recipe, photograph, mention, and nudge. I appreciate your confidence in me, and hope to keep sharing all the amazing food, adventures, stories and locales Arkansas has to offer.

Buttermilk Pie

5. eggs
2. cups sugar
1. stick butter or oleo
1. cup Buttermilk
1. tbsp. lemon juice
1. tsp. vanilla
2. tbsp. flour

Blend butter, sugar, then add remaining ingredients & blend until well. Pour into unbaked 9 in pie shell & bake at 325. Requires 9 in Pie Shell. Makes 1 thick & 1 thin pie.

BUTTERMILK PIE

1 1/3 cup sugar
3. tbsp. flour
2. eggs beaten
1/2. cup butter or oleo
1. cup buttermilk
2. tsp. vanilla extract
1. tsp. lemon extract
1-unbaked 9 inch pastry shell

combine sugar & flour, mix well
add eggs, butter & buttermilk. beat well. stir in flavorings. pour
into pastry shell. bake at 400 for 10 min. then bake at 350 for 30
to 40 min. yield 1 thick pie & 1 thin pie.

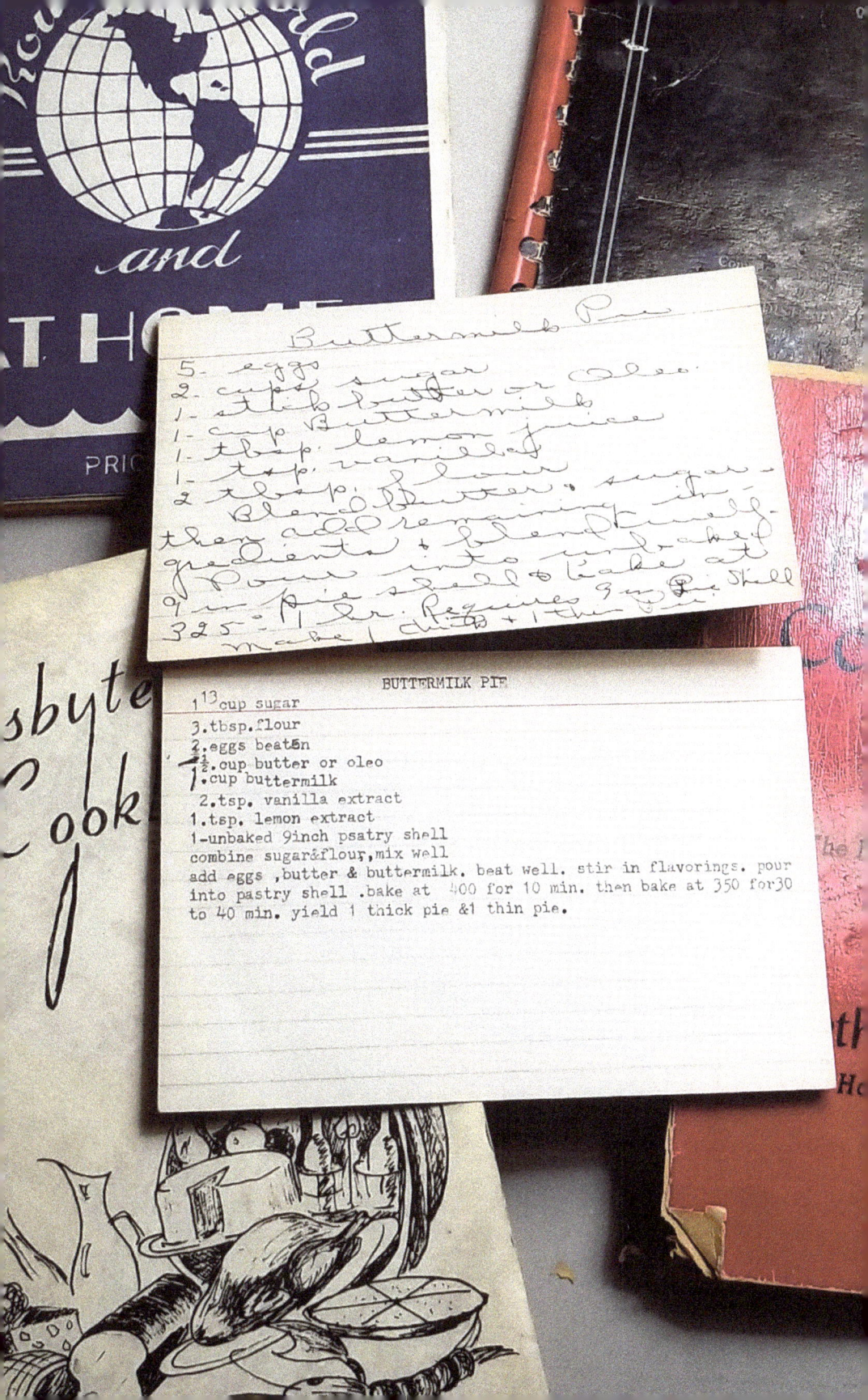

INTRODUCTION

Why things are the way things are...

When I was a Girl Scout, somewhere maybe 4th or 5th grade, my troop visited a nursing home over the holidays We had made spice sachets for the residents, and were encouraged to spend time chatting with a couple of these older folks, to learn about them.

I remember sitting with a delightful lady with an unreasonably (for the time) shade of blue in her hair. I wish I could remember her name. I do remember sitting and looking through a scrapbook with her, except this wasn't like a scrapbook of just photos but of things, like dried flowers preserved with Scotch tape, newspaper articles, bits of ribbon, and handwritten notes. And there were recipes in there, in several different hands. She talked to me about the different recipes. Boy, I wish my ten- or eleven-year-old self could have recorded better what she said, because it was certainly priceless information.

I remember clearly giving her a green sachet It was made from a tie that had come to the troop somehow. I'd practiced stitching on it and learned how to make it so that it was one long folded over piece - over once to secure all the edges, then folded like an omelet one and two, so that the edges overlapped on one side, sewing the seams down both sides, turning it inside out. I also remember all of us putting the spices in the coffee filters and tying ribbon to keep it closed, slipping it in the tiny pillow... and how, with a sniff, that lady told me everything in the sachet, that Christmas sachet, the allspice and cloves and cinnamon, and her telling me why you didn't use whole nutmeg. She knew without feeling about in the little pocket, without hardly touching, with just smell alone, what was in there. And she told me I could train myself to do that, too.

And I remember, looking at the recipes, asking her why tablespoon had a big T and teaspoon had a little t. And she told me, you won't mess up the measurements if you know what they are.

It wasn't a secret, though maybe I thought I was, standing there in my green slacks and sash and red tie. It was a shorthand that was taken as a given, that I have now found again and again and again on those handwritten recipes I've encountered,

Introduction

tucked into old cookbooks or stuck in the back end of a forgotten cabinet. Big T for tablespoon and you'll never go wrong. Some recipes literally have "2 T sg" and I know that's two tablespoons of sugar.

So in my cookbook, I've standardized things a bit. I have no worry for column inches or typing on an old school Underwood 5 where correction tape is a pain in the batookis to place and erase, so I write the full words out. Years as a reader makes this so much more comfortable for me, and leaves no room for ambiguity. I've included, or at least made the attempt to, indicate on every recipe what sort of pie crust to use, if any at all, because so many of our older cookbook contributors just make the assumption you know what's on their mind. I've updated the measurements to reflect a world where we've gone from three ounce tabs of cream cheese to eight ounce blocks, replaced Oleo and margarine references with butter, updated cans of coconut with ounces that come in bags. And wherever you see tablespoon in a list of ingredients, you'll see a capital T. As I grow older and my eyes lose their reliability, just catching the difference in case is enough to avoid a kitchen escapade or failure or, as I've ended up doing when I've missed a notation before, doubled or tripled my recipe to account for my miscounting and misreading of things.

Yes, you can train yourself to tell what spices are in a sachet, or a pie, or any dish, really. You can collect recipes and watch other people for years make dishes, but until you get into the kitchen and spend time with flour under your nails (and in your hair, and your pockets), there's still an adventure to be had, and as I've learned, one I can share.

...

My mom's house burned to the ground on May 4, 2022. I was, at the time, struggling to figure out where my place was going to be in the world again. When the pandemic shut everything down, I turned inwards, wrote cookbooks, delved into memories, spent time with my daughter, and slowly released the drive that had been so very consuming since I'd devoted my career to restaurant writing and Arkansas food promotion. I put a couple of cookbooks under my belt, had shoulder surgery that took so very long from which to heal, and just when I was thinking I needed to do anything I could to get back out in the world, the dairy bars project took me. Except for the two weeks in July 2021 where I cooked all the things for *Arkansas Cookery*, and the couple of weeks that October where I sewed that book together, dairy bars were everything. I spent three weeks shooting the show, six weeks editing video, another week editing it down further, and on both sides of that six months writing and photographing for and laying out that book. When it was all done, I had nothing left in my hands to write. With eight books in four years, I needed a break.

So I took a little one. I cleared my head, and about the time my daughter finally started attending in-person school again, I got back out on the road. I had just completed a whirlwind run through touring all the new stuff that had come online in Bentonville, picking up assignment work in south Arkansas and pushing through the second Arkansas Pie Festival. And then that call came.

I can't really touch what was going through my head, those days after, holding that figurative wake sitting at the lone surviving cast iron table, talking to inspectors and adjusters while the fire still crackled. I made the conscious decision to take time off to help my mom get through things. Then I helped my partner push his business further towards its success. I'd sometimes go take a look on social media and got that whole FOMO as I saw what other local food writers were doing, but I let it go for a time. It didn't matter.

Funny thing, though. I thought my time away from the constant push to promote our foodways would mean folks would forget and move on to whomever the next hot flavor is in this crazy editorial world. They didn't though. The messages asking for restaurant recommendations kept coming. Folks kept stopping me at the store to tell me about watching one of the shows on PBS, or about how a relative had responded to receiving a book. And everyone seemed to have the same question: *what are you going to do next?*

I don't have any photographs of most of my family. Most of what I have, happens to be things we took photos of so we could share on social media. Most of the dishes we cooked in (an errant Blue Cornflower Corningware pie plate was at my house) were gone, furniture my great-grandfather made, artwork from my school days... all ashes. Things I thought could be recovered, we would find, metal crumbling, porcelain shattered, books all but evaporated.

Families lose bits all the time. But those portions we find we haven't lost, we keep. We hold them dear. Maybe my mom's mother and I didn't get along so well. She couldn't really understand me and when I was younger I lacked the desire to find a point of relevance for us both. But I can remember those jars of mincemeat on the shelves and what those pies tasted like.

Introduction

Diners are like that, too. They may have a hard time recalling the name of the person who made the pie at that one restaurant they liked 20, 40 years ago, but they can tell you what that pie tasted like, and know it intrinsically. Those flavors of our days, those scents, those memories, we try to hold onto them any way we can.

In 2012, my very first book, *Arkansas Pie: A Delicious Slice of The Natural State*, came out with its burgeoning essays and Grav Weldon's photographs and just 13 recipes within - just enough to make folks mad. In 2018, when faced with that book being out of print, I scrambled for 10 weeks and scurried up *Another Slice of Arkansas Pie*, a guide which told hungry folks where to find all those great homemade pies anywhere around these parts, all 475 of them at the time. This time, I've put together what was missing between those two books. I've spent more than a decade collecting recipes for this project, and in the course of the last six months I've reached out and gathered even more. I've also dug into my collection of (now) more than 500 Arkansas church and community cookbooks, compared what most have in common and pulled out so many to try. Over the course of two different two week sessions at The Writers' Colony at Dairy Hollow in Eureka Springs, I've tested close to 100 of them, photographed them, and prepared them to sit alongside those provided by both home cooks and professionals I've encountered during my 16 year sojourn researching Arkansas foodways.

Honestly, my pies can be pretty ugly. No doubt, there are few places where my ugly double crusted fruit pies could sit alongside those by kitchen magicians such as KJ Zumwalt and Margaret Burris, nor could my thin and gnarly browned meringues hold a finger to Alma French's Mile High Pies or the gorgeous meringue swells perched on pies like Sharon Woodson, Anne Wood, or Paul or Abbie Frintrup. But overall, each of these pies is a larger part of a whole story, a love story to our palates, to our affection for pastry-clad delights. It's an ancient affectation, reflected in diner menu boards today and a century ago, in those chicken and wild game pies of centuries back, even in our proto-pumpkin pies from our Italian and French ancestors and roasted pumpkins with milk and honey from our Native American forefathers and mothers.

All this to say, this book is a result of its time in my life and in our place in Arkansas food history. The pies may be from different decades and different centuries but they are timeless. So too is this book, I hope, as I await holding it in my hands come the end of April, when we'll put on the third Arkansas Pie Festival in Cherokee Village. Savor these bites within, enjoy the flavor of this moment, and may what you read here make you hungry and yet satisfied.

Kat Robinson
April 8, 2023
Little Rock

CRUST TYPES

CRUSTS

Many of the pies within this book come with their own particular crust recipe. But in general, the recipes we wee in our older cookbooks are for pie fillings. Sometimes there's a call in the recipe for a particular type of crust - be it pastry, graham racker, or ginger snap. Whether that crust is baked in advance or not, can make a great deal of difference in the way pies come out.

Over the course of two separate two week sessions, I went back to the drawing board on crusts. I have long made my own, preferring a hand-patted butter crust to rolled crusts or making a crust with other fats. To me, if I was going to truly tackle making a pie from scratch, I needed to understand how crusts worked, and what method I liked best. I also wanted to consider how a crust would have been made before refrigeration, with different sorts of fats, and with different materials available.

What I came to find was that there are just some days I can't make a crust right to save my life. There was one particular Thursday in February where I made one ball of fail after another, never getting the right amount of liquid into the flour or working it way too much. With fillings prepared and an oven ready to accept the pies to come, I found myself frustrated with the heat of an overwhelmed kitchen and the pressure of so many pies to be made. At the end of that day, I went to dinner, came back to my room and went right to bed at 7:15 in the evening, feeling a total failure.

The next day, everything kicked into place. When the room got hot, I opened the door and let the wind in. I stopped being stingy with the water I was adding to the dough. And I went back to a recipe that a colleague of mine at Serious Eats developed, and went from there. In fact, J. Kenji López-Alt's easy pie recipe wasn't just the moment I felt crust-accomplished; it came back to me in submitted recipes again and again. Using the weight of the flour rather than volume was an insight I should have followed long before.

Another difference with my crusts came in my upper body strength and memories of baking throughout my life. When

Crust Types

given a roller, I found that I tend to roll nearly translucent doughs at time, using about half of what the recipes called for. While this did create a crust, it wasn't sturdy enough for my needs. So I thought in the way my brain works, I would roll two crusts for one, lightly buttering the lower layer before dropping the upper layer on. It's probably not what most people would have done, but... *shrugs* that's just how it worked for me.

There were, of course, other crusts. There was sandy-bottom crusts, which I found were really magnificent when substituting almond flour or pecan flour for half the wheat flour in the recipe. There was making graham cracker crusts and chocolate cookie crusts and Oreo cookie crusts and figuring out how to make the crust stick without, well, sticking. I played with meringue crusts and saltines.

And then I played with fats, first with the more forgiving vegetable shortening and then with animal fats, finely chopped brisket fat from a fatty end Grav Weldon smoked for me, ground beef and steak fats rendered during cooking, and my favorite of all - schmaltz. The latter, I spent days procuring, first collecting the fats dripped from roasting ten pounds of chicken leg quarters, then pulling the fats from the top of another ten pounds of chicken boiled down with mirepoix and spices to make up what came to be just a few cups of good, solid schmaltz. This crust gave me the most joy overall, which I'll share when we get to the savory pie chapter.

I won't shame anyone who chooses to use a pre-packaged pie crust or a powdered mix - there are reasons these products exist, with the top reason being time. My eyes have been opened, though, and now that I've worked my way through dozens of pounds of flour, I have my favorites.

SERIOUS EATS PASTRY CRUST

There is the question: why re-invent the wheel? J. Kenji López-Alt's pie crust recipe for Serious Eats has been referenced by so many of the home cooks and chefs I've consulted while working on this book. Measuring by weight instead of volume does indeed often have an effect on how a crust comes out. This is the revised version for this book.

2-3/4 cup (12.5 ounces, 350g) all-purpose flour, divided
2 Tablespoons (25g) sugar
1-1/2 teaspoon (5g) kosher salt or same weight by volume table salt
2-1/2 sticks (10 ounces, 280g) unsalted butter, sliced to 1/4 inch
6 Tablespoons (3 ounces, 85ml) cold water

Combine two thirds of flour with sugar and salt in the bowl of a food processor. Pulse twice to incorporate. Spread butter slices evenly over surface. Pulse until no dry flour remains and dough just begins to collect in clumps, about 25 short pulses. Use a rubber spatula to spread the dough evenly around the bowl of the food processor. Sprinkle with remaining flour and pulse until dough is just barely broken up, about 5 short pulses. Transfer dough to a large bowl.

Sprinkle with water. Then, using a rubber spatula, fold and press dough until it comes together into a ball. Divide ball in half. Form each half into a roughly 4-inch disk. Wrap tightly in plastic and refrigerate for at least 2 hours before rolling and baking.

When ready to shape the dough, pull out one ball, set it on a well-floured work surface, and sprinkle with more flour. Use a tapered rolling pin to start rolling the dough out into a circle, lifting the dough and rotating it while rolling to achieve an even shape. Continue rolling, changing the angle of your rolling pin as you go to get an even shape and thickness. The finished dough should overhang your pie plate by an inch or two.

Pick up the dough by carefully rolling it around your rolling pin, using your bench scraper to help lift it off the work surface. Unroll it over a pie plate. Gently lift and fit the dough into the pie plate, getting down into the corners.

For a single-crusted pie, use a pair of scissors to trim the dough so that it overhangs the edge by 1/2 inch all around. For a double-crusted pie, at this stage, fill it and drape your second round of pie dough over the top. Trim it to a 1/2-inch overhang along with the lower crust. Either way, tuck the overhanging edge(s) under itself all the way around the pie.

Crust Types

ALL BUTTER PIE CRUST

This recipe from Blue Cake Honey Pies is an easy go-to that's quick and can be frozen and stored for later use. This dough makes two single crusts or one double crust and produces 24 ounces of dough.

3 cups (12 ounces) all-purpose flour
2 Tablespoon (1 ounce) granulated sugar
1 teaspoon kosher salt
2 and 1/2 sticks (10 ounces) butter, cold
2 Tablespoons + 2 teaspoons cold water

Combine dry ingredients in mixing bowl. Blend thoroughly. Grate cold butter into dry ingredients. Combine and mix for a sandy texture. Add water and mix just until combined.

Turn dough onto lightly floured surface; flatten and fold until cohesive dough forms, but do not overmix! Flatten into disc and chill for at least 30 minutes or until cold. For best results, allow to rest overnight so flour can fully hydrate.

Roll 12 ounces of dough to line a deep-dish 9" pie tin.

To blind bake; line chilled pie shell with foil or plastic wrap and fill with dried beans, rice or pie weights. Bake at 375° for 12-15 minutes, or shell is set. Remove pie weights and return to oven until pie shell is dry but not browned.

PATTY'S PASTRY DOUGH

A different take on the all-butter crust, this is the dough used for pies at Nellie B's in Elkins. It makes one double or two single crusts.

2 cups all-purpose flour
1 teaspoon salt
1 cup minus 2 Tablespoons butter
5 Tablespoons cold water
1 cup flour for rolling dough

Place flour, salt, and butter into a bowl. Using a pastry cutter, blend in butter until mixture is pea sized crumbs. Begin with folding in 2 tablespoons cold water, adding 1 tablespoon at a time until the mixture is soft and clings together.

Flour your hands and pastry board. Mold the pastry dough in your hands into a ball and then cut in half. Place half the dough on the board and wrap the other half in plastic. Set aside.

Flatten the dough on the board slightly, and roll into a circle about 1/4 larger than your pie pan.

Place crust in the pan and form decorative edges with your then and forefingers. If using a double crust pie, place the crust in the pan and fill with pie filling. Roll out second half of pie dough to match the first in size, place over filling and crimp decorative edges all around.

Hot Water Pie Crust

½ cup water, boiling
1 cup shortening
½ teaspoon salt
3 cups flour, sifted

Stir water and shortening together until creamy. Add salt and stir to blend. Sift flour into large mixing bowl. Add shortening mixture to flour, stirring to blend. Chill until firm. Roll out very thin when ready to use. Excellent for freezing!

Mary Waldon

This is my maternal grandmother's pie crust recipe, as printed in *Cornerstone Cookery*.

Homemade Pie Crust
(For one single crust)

1 cup all purp. flour } Sift
1/4 teasp. salt   } into bowl

- Cut 1/3 cup Vegtable shortening into flour until it is mealy & crumbly.

Sprinkle 3 Tablespoons orange juice over the flour mixture & mix until it holds together.

- Roll out on floured surface or pat out in pie pan (9") prick the bottom. (For cream pies)

Bake at 375° until golden - (start checking on after 10 minutes)

HOMEMADE VEGETABLE SHORTENING PIE CRUST

This crust recipe from DeVito's Restaurant in Bear Creek Springs uses vegetable shortening instead of butter.

1 and 1/3 cups all-purpose flour
1/2 teaspoon salt
1/2 stick or 1/2 cup vegetable shortening
3 Tablespoons cold water

Mix flour and salt in medium bowl. Cut in shortening using pastry blender or two knives until all flour is blended to form pea-sized chunks. Sprinkle with water, one tablespoon at a time. Toss lightly with a fork until dough ball forms.

Press dough ball between hands to form a 5-6 inch pancake. Four dough lightly. Roll into circle between two pieces of wax paper on dampened countertop. Peel off top sheet of wax paper. Trim dough one inch larger than inverted 9-inch pie plate. Flip into pie plate. Remove other sheet of wax paper and press pastry to fit. Fold edge under and flute.

GLUTEN-FREE ALL BUTTER PIE CRUST

This recipe is utilized at Dogwood Hills Guest Farm, which keeps an entirely gluten-free kitchen for its guests. You'll find recipes in these pages for a brown sugar buttermilk pie on page 126, and a cannoli pie on page 132, both of which are completely gluten-free as long as you use this crust.

1/2 cup cold butter
1-1/2 cup Bob's Red Mill Gluten-Free All-Purpose Baking Flour
1/2 teaspoon salt
4-6 Tablespoons cold milk

Cube butter and freeze for one hour. Combine flour and salt, then cut in butter using a pastry cutter or food processor until the mixture resembles coarse meal. Sprinkle cold milk, one tablespoon at a time, mixing everything with a dough scraper to hydrate the dough. Form dough into disk, wrap in plastic, and refrigerate one hour.

Place chilled dough on plastic wrap, then top with more plastic wrap and roll to the desired size. Remove top sheet, invert on pie pan, remove remaining sheet and shape as desired. Freeze 15 minutes before removing to bake.

Heat oven to 400°. Bake 15-20 minutes to blind bake.

FAT FREE PIE CRUST

This recipe comes from the *Carnegie Public Library Cookbook II* from Eureka Springs

1-1/2 cups Grape-Nuts cereal
2 ounces apple juice
1/2 teaspoon cinnamon

Combine the ingredients and mix thoroughly. Press firmly into a 9 inch pie plate and bake at 425° for about 12 minutes.

STANDARD PIE CRUST

Billy Joe Tatum and Ann Taylor Packer's 1987 book *The Ozark Collection: The Best Recipes fro the Heritage and Traditions of a Storied Region* is a deep dive into the history of what we eat in portions of our state. From that book:

> **The crust of a pie may be just the receptacle to hold the pie filling, or it may be an integral part of the total finished product, or it may be itself a complimentary tasty treat.**

2 cups flour
1/2 teaspoon salt
2/3 cup shortening, preferably chilled
6 Tablespoons cold water, or as needed

Combine salt and flour in a large bowl. Cut in shortening until mixture has the texture of cornmeal. Sprinkle cold water over mixture a little at a time, stirring with a fork until dough is just moist enough to hold together when squeezed. Form a ball and divide in half. Roll thin on floured board. Makes enough for two single or one double pastry crust.

Pastry variations
For an extra-flaky crust use the standard crust recipe, pat out, brush with oil, fold in half, brush again with oil. Fold in fourths and roll out to fit the pan. Add cinnamon and a bit of sugar to the standard recipe for a spicy crust particularly suitable for pumpkin, persimmon or apple pie. Nuts pressed into the crust after rolling are good with any pie containing nuts or for pumpkin or persimmon.

The Great Arkansas Pie Book

This is Evelyn Weldon's pie crust recipe.

> Recipe for: **Pie Crust**
> from the kitchen of: _____
>
> 3 C. Flour } Mix in a
> 1 C. Shortening } mixer until crumbly
>
> In a 1 C. measure beat 1 egg + 1 T. vinegar add enough water to measure ½ C. Pour mixture into flour + mix until all flour is mixed w/ mixer.
>
> _____ serves: _____

GOOSEBERRY HANDMADE PIES LARD CRUST

Out of all the different restaurants and bakeries I've visited across Arkansas, there's only one that admits to using a lard crust in their pies. It may come as no small wonder that the place is Gooseberry Handmade Pies The father-daughter team of Paul and Abbie Frintrup are producing a finely curated, small-bakery production of gorgeously decorated heritage recipe pies. This is the dough to use for the Chocolate Italian Meringue recipe on page 194 - or any pie you'd like to sample utilizing lard.

310 grams flour
8 grams sugar (optional)
4 grams salt
227 grams lard
1/2 cup (120ml) cold water

Combine flour, sugar (if using), salt and lard in a bowl. Cut in using a pastry cutter until the mixture is crumbly. Slowly drizzle water over the flour mixture and gently mix until the dough comes together. Divide dough in half and roll one portion to a 12 inch diameter and place into a pie tin. Place the filling of your choice inside the pie plate, and the other rolled dough on top. Roll and crimp the edges. Using a sharp knife, cut vent holes in the top of the pie.

FRUIT PIES

1829 LEMON PIE

This recipe dates back to 1829. A version comes to this cookbook from its inclusion in the *Alexander Human Development Center Volunteer Council Cookbook* printed in 1981, and is attributed to Opal DePriest.

2 lemons, sliced paper thin, including rind
2 heaping cups sugar
4 eggs, well beaten
1 unbaked 9 inch pastry pie crust

Remove seeds from lemons during slicing process. Reserve all juice. Place in bowl and cover with sugar. Allow to sit at least two hours or up to overnight, stirring occasionally.

Heat oven to 300°. Fold eggs into lemon sugar mixture and pour into pie crust. Shield pie edges. Bake for one hour or until top is golden brown. Allow to completely cool before serving.

Fruit Pies

APPLE RAISIN NUT PIE

This recipe comes from Mrs. Tom J Cowan, published in *Our Daily Bread: A Book of Favorite Recipes* by the Women of First Presbyterian Church, Morrilton, in 1995. I like using walnuts in this version for their meatiness. I'm also not so great with lattice, as you see by my 1.5 inch wide pastry strips here.

- 6 to 8 apples
- 3/4 cup raisins
- 2/3 cup sugar
- 1/4 teaspoon salt
- 1 teaspoon cinnamon
- 1/4 teaspoon nutmeg
- 1/2 cup water
- 1 Tablespoon cornstarch
- 3/4 cup chopped nuts
- 2 unbaked 9 inch pastry pie crusts

Peel, core and slice apples. Combine with raisins, sugar, salt, spices, and water. Cook together for 10 minutes. Thicken mixture with cornstarch dissolved in a little cold water. Add nuts and pour into pie pan lined with pastry. Cover top with strips of pastry, cut half inch wide and put on in lattice fashion. Put in hot oven (425° F) for first 10 minutes, then reduce heat to 350° and bake until crown is browned.

29

APPLE PIE

I first met KJ Zumwalt at the extraordinary restaurant she owned in Eureka Springs, a colorful place called Caribe. Though the restaurant is now a memory, we've stayed friends. She's always encouraged me, and has gifted me this recipe from Joan R. Zumwalt, her mom, for a glorious apple pie. The inclusion of both tart and sweet apples is key.

4-3 red apples (Pink Ladies, Red Delicious or the like)
4-5 Granny Smith apples
1 stick (4 ounces) salted butter
3 Tablespoons flour
1/2 cup brown sugar
1;2 cup white sugar
1/4 cup water
2 unbaked 9 inch pastry pie crusts (see below)

Heat oven to 425°. Place bottom crust in a Dutch oven. Peel and core all apples and slice thin. Place apples in the crust with careful layering, mounding in the center. Cut remaining crust in strips and lattice over apples.

Heat butter in saucepan and dust with flour. Stir! Cook about 3-4 minutes but do not let stick. Add a bit of water only if needed. Add both sugars and stir. Finally, add the water and stir, stir, stir!

While still piping hot, spoon liquid over pie, filling all the squares in the lattice. Use all of the liquid.

Bake 15 minutes at 425°, then reduce heat to 350° and bake an additional 40 minutes, making sure crust is golden. Let cool, then slice and serve with vanilla ice cream.

MAMA JO'S FLAKY CRUST

2-1/4 cups flour
1-1/2 teaspoon salt
1/3 cup cold milk
1/2 cup and 1 Tablespoon salad oil

Mix flour and salt. Pour milk and oil into same measuring cup - do not stir. Add all at once to flour. Stir with a fork until well mixed.

Press dough into ball. Divide. Roll out between sheets of wax paper.

Fruit Pies

BLACK AND BLUE BERRY PIE

This recipe from Marilyn Foltz Whisenhant was included in *Another Slice of Arkansas Pie: A Guide to the Best Restaurants, Bakeries, Truck Stops and Food Trucks for Delectable Bites in The Natural State*, under the name Maine Black and Blue Berry Pie.

3 cups blueberries, rinsed and dried
3 cups blackberries, rinsed and dried
¼ cup to 1 cup sugar, depending on tartness of berries
1 teaspoon grated lemon zest
3 Tablespoons cornstarch
1/4 cup heavy cream
2 unbaked 9 inch pastry pie crusts
1 egg white, beaten with 1 teaspoon water
sugar

Preheat oven to 425°. Line pie plate with pastry. In a large bowl combine berries, sugar, cornstarch and lemon zest. Toss gently to mix. Spoon filling into pastry shell. Dampen rime of pastry with a little of the egg white mixture. Cover with the top pastry. Cut an 8 inch X in the center. Fold back points from center and seal triangle points to pastry with egg white mixture to create a square in the center of the pie. Fold under and crimp edges. Brush top with remaining egg mixture and sprinkle with sugar.

Place foil or drip pan on oven rack below pie. Bake 15 minutes at 425° then lower oven temperature to 350°. Cover pie lightly with foil and bake 30 minutes more. Spoon the heavy cream into the center. Return pie to oven and bake 15 minutes longer.

Fruit Pies

BLUEBERRY STRAWBERRY PIE

This recipe was redacted from one for strawberry pie by Neal Hart in the 1970 book *Cook's Delight* by the Victory Baptist Elementary Parent Teacher Fellowship. I augmented by replacing half the strawberries called for with blueberries.

1 pound frozen strawberries
1 pound frozen blueberries
1/2 teaspoon lemon juice
2 Tablespoons cornstarch
1.4 teaspoon salt
1 cup juice drained from defrosted fruit (add water to equal 1 cup if necessary)
1/4 cup sugar
1 baked 9 inch pastry pie crust
whipped cream for garnish

Defrost fruit in package. Drain juice from fruit. Sprinkle lemon juice over fruit. Blend cornstarch, salt and sugar in saucepan. Stir in fruit juice. Cook, stirring constantly, until thickened. Let cool. Arrange fruit in pie crust. Pour cooled sauce over fruit. Chill at least three hours in refrigerator. Garnish with whipped cream.

BLUEBERRY PIE

This is my personal blueberry pie recipe. I love the flavor of lemon with blueberry, and this works really well together. The secret? A handful of white chocolate chips.

1 baked 9 inch pastry pie crust
4 ounces white chocolate chips
3/4 cup sugar
1 teaspoon unflavored gelatin
1/4 teaspoon salt
1/4 cup cold water
5 cups fresh blueberries, divided
1 Tablespoon butter
1 Tablespoon lemon juice

Heat oven to 350°. Pour white chocolate chips into previously baked pie shell. Bake for 10 minutes, then remove from oven and allow to cool.

In a saucepan over medium heat, combine sugar, gelatin, salt and water until smooth. Add 3 cups blueberries. Bring to a boil; cook and stir for 2 minutes or until thickened and bubbly.

Remove from heat. Add butter, lemon juice and remaining berries. Stir til butter is melted. Cool. Pour into crust. Refrigerate.

BROWN BAG APPLE PIE

I have to admit, approaching this recipe made me nervous. See, I've heard of people baking pies and even turkeys in brown paper bags in the oven before. I also have experiences with oven fires, and the very idea makes me nervous. There was also the search for brown paper bags; many of our grocery stores around these parts have stopped using them altogether. Fortunately, the folks at Hart's Grocery in Eureka Springs obliged with the necessary equipment, and I was delighted to taste this excellent, perfectly cooked pie, which both steamed the apples and kept the crust from burning.

4 medium apples, chopped (at least two different varieties)
1/2 cup sugar
2 Tablespoons flour
1/2 teaspoon nutmeg
2 Tablespoons lemon juice
1 unbaked 9 inch pastry pie crust

Combine sugar, flour and nutmeg. Toss apples in flour mixture. Lay into pie shell and sprinkle with lemon juice.

1/2 cup sugar
1/2 cup flour
1/2 cup butter
1/2 teaspoon salt

Heat oven to 425°. Cut butter into sugar, flour and salt. Sprinkle over apples. Slide pie into paper bag, being careful not to break pastry edges with sides. Fold over end and clip or staple. Slide into oven. Bake for one hour.

CARAMEL BOTTOM PEACH PIE

My friend Ashley Lavender shared this lovely recipe with me for *Another Slice of Arkansas Pie: A Guide to the Best Restaurants, Bakeries, Truck Stops and Food Trucks for Delectable Bites in The Natural State*. It's a really good summertime pie.

2 Tablespoons butter
2 Tablespoons flour
3/4 cup evaporated milk
1 cup sugar
1/2 teaspoon salt

1 deep dish pie crust
2 cups fresh peaches
   (about 6-7 medium peaches)
1 baked 9 inch pastry pie crust
16 ounces whipped topping

Make a paste over the stove with the butter and flour. Add in 3/4 cups evaporated milk, then the sugar and salt. Heat until thickened. Pour into baked pie crust Refrigerate one hour.

Skin and slice peaches and fold into two thirds of the whipped topping. Add to caramel-filled crust. Top with remaining whipped topping. Refrigerate until ready to serve.

Fruit Pies

CARAMEL CRUNCH APPLE PIE

Pickles Gap Village graced a curve north of Conway for decades, with shops offering crafts, knives, furniture and fudge. In 1997, Janis Mack published *All Day Singin' and Dinner on the Grounds Cookbook: A Southern Tradition*, full of classic local recipes including a number of pies. I'm a big fan of this one, which isn't too sweet with a lovely crunch. Use two or three types of apples for best results.

24 caramels (about 1/2 a 14 ounce bag), unwrapped
2 Tablespoons water
4 cups apples, peeled and sliced
3/4 cups flour
1/3 cup sugar
1/2 teaspoon ground cinnamon
1/3 cup butter
1/2 cup walnuts, chopped
1 unbaked 9 inch pastry crust

Melt caramels with water in heavy saucepan over low heat, stirring frequently until smooth. Spoon apples into crust; top with caramel sauce. Mix flour, sugar and cinnamon. Cut in butter until mixture resembles coarse crumbs. Stir in walnuts. Sprinkle mixture over apples. Bake in preheated 375° oven for 40-45 minutes or until apples are tender.

This is excellent with whipped cream.

CHERRY MINI PIES or HAND PIES

Blue Cake Honey Pies may have an unusual name - being the combination of famed Blue Cake Company and Honey Pies, two fantastic pastry shops in Little Rock - but the pies they create are both beautiful and tasty. This recipe can be used for fold-over handpies or for small lattice pies. It's a great topping for cream cheese pies, too.

16 ounces frozen tart or blend of cherries *or* pitted fresh cherries
2/3 cup (6 ounces) sugar
3 Tablespoons cornstarch
One recipe All Butter Pie Crust (see page 21)

Combine cherries, sugar and cornstarch in wide saucepan. Cook, stirring constantly, until mixture bubbles for one minute. Cool.

Portion pie crust into 8 three-ounce balls. Roll between wax paper or cut from dough to create 6" disks.

For hand pies, portion filling onto half of disk, fold over and crimp to seal. Cut 2-3 small vents.

For mini pies, line pie tins. Trim edges. Fill with pie filling. Top with desired design (double crust with vent, lattice, etc.).

For both application, brush with egg wash and sprinkle with granulated sugar. Chill or freeze until dough is rested and firm, at least 20 minutes. Bake at 375° until crust is golden brown and filling is bubbly, approximately 20-25 minutes.

CHERRY PIE

The venerable Sue's Pie Shop, a jewel in Little Rock's Heights district, was always a sure bet for excellent pies for any occasion. Though the place has long since transitioned to a series of other businesses, Sue Lopes continues to share her recipes through occasional cooking classes and her 1991 book, *Sue's Pie Shop: Collection of Recipes by Sue Lopez*.

1 cup sugar + more for sprinkling
3 Tablespoons flour
1/4 teaspoon salt
1/4 teaspoon red food coloring
1-14.5 ounce can tart pitted cherries, with juice
2 tablespoons butter
2 unbaked pastry pie crusts

Place one pastry pie crust into a nine inch pan. Mix sugar, flour and salt together. Add cherries with juice and food coloring and mix well. Pour into unbaked pie shell. Dot with butter. Cut strips from second pie crust and make a lattice top on pie. Seal edges and sprinkle with sugar. Bake in 425° oven for 10 minutes, then reduce temperature to 350° and bake 20 minutes more or until filling begins to bubble.

CHERRY PIE

Mayonnaise? In a cherry pie? That's what you'll find in this recipe from Robin Welch found in *Sunday Best*, a 1986 Little Rock cookbook by Calvary Baptist Church, a nice new touch on an old classic.

1 graham cracker pie crust
1 egg yolk, slightly beaten
1-21 ounce can cherry pie filling
  (or filling for cherry pie, page 38)
3/4 cup unsifted flour
1/2 cup sugar
1/4 teaspoon ground cinnamon
1/3 cup mayonnaise

Heat oven to 400°. Brush bottom and sides of prepared graham cracker crust with egg yolk. Place on baking sheet and bake 3-5 minutes or until the crust begins to brown. Spoon filling into crust. In separate bowl, stir together flour, sugar and cinnamon. Cut in mayonnaise with pastry cutter or two knives until it resembles coarse crumbs. Sprinkle over pie filling. Bake 30-35 minutes or until crumbs are golden brown.

COMPANY APPLE PIE

This particular recipe appears in dozens of Arkansas cookbooks through the 1980s and 90s. It differs from the traditional apple pie by using sour cream instead of lemon juice in its filling This exact recipe comes from Dolores Benton and appears in *Camden's Back on Track: The Shared Recipes of Camden, Arkansas Cooks in Support of the Missouri Pacific Depot Restoration*, printed in 1995.

1 deep dish pastry pie crust

Filling
1 cup sugar
1/2 cup flour
1 teaspoon vanilla
1 deep-dish pie crust
1 cup sour cream
1 egg
8 apples, peeled, cored and sliced

Topping:
1/2 cup walnuts
1/2 cup sugar
3/4 cups flour
1 tablespoon cinnamon
1/2 cup butter
1/2 cup brown sugar

Set oven to 400°. Blend sugar, sour cream, flour, egg and vanilla until smooth; add apples and pour into pie shell. Bake for 45 minutes or until apples are tender. Mix together all topping ingredients; sprinkle evenly over top of pie and bake 15 minutes longer.

RUBY TUESDAY APPLE PIE

When this recipe was sent to me several years back, I laughed hard and long, before it hit me - sometimes you just gotta cut the corners you can and move on. For your enjoyment.

1 frozen double crust deep dish apple pie
2 sticks butter
1 cup light brown sugar
3-1/2 teaspoons cinnamon
1/4 teaspoon allspice
1/4 teaspoon ground cloves
1-1/2 teaspoon lemon juice
3/4 cup flour
1/2 cup sugar
1-1/3 cup chopped walnuts

Let pie thaw at room table for one hour. Make an X in the center of the crust with a sharp knife and carefully pull back each corner. Heat oven to 350°. Melt one stick of butter in saucepan over medium heat. Add half the brown sugar, 1 1/2 teaspoons cinnamon, and the allspice, cloves and lemon juice. Stir well until sugar is dissolved. Pour into hole in crust and then turn the crust back over, leaving the slits from the X. Bake for 30 minutes. Remove from oven and reduce heat to 325°. Make an aluminum foil ring around the edge of the pie to hold additional topping. Mix together remaining ingredients and spread over pie. Bake an additional 30-40 minutes. Serve with ice cream.

Fruit Pies

ENGLISH APPLE PIE

Vesta Pryor, a fifth grade teacher, put together the original recipe but without some key instructions. I've added them, and suggest preparing it in a layered double pie crust for maximum effect.

Pastry for double crust pie
1 cup sugar
1 egg, beaten well
1 cup flour
1/2 teaspoon nutmeg
1 teaspoon cinnamon
1 teaspoon baking soda
1/2 teaspoon salt
2-1/2 cups apples, chopped
3/4 cups walnuts or pecans, chopped
Egg wash for crust

Heat oven to 350°. Cream together sugar and butter, then add egg. Sift together flour and spices. Toss together with apples and nuts. Combine with other ingredients. Lay bottom crust into 9 inch pie plate, trimming to 1 inch overlap. Spoon filling into pan. Top with second crust, tucking top crust into bottom crust. Brush with egg wash and vent. Bake for one hour.

FRENCH AMARETTO PEACH PIE

Daisy's Lunchbox in Searcy is well known and loved for its chicken salad and the second largest cinnamon rolls in the state. Their pies and tarts are darling and delicious. Suzanne Raiford shares this delightful recipe for a much-demanded pie in the rotation at Daisy's.

1 large can sliced peaches, drained
1 stick butter
1 cup sugar
2 eggs
2 teaspoons amaretto liqueur
2 and a half Tablespoons flour
1 unbaked 9 inch pastry pie crust

Place drained peaches in pie shell. In bowl, mix butter, sugar, eggs, amaretto and flour. Beat well, then pour over the peaches. Bake one hour at 300°.

Fruit Pies

FRENCH APPLE PIE

This recipe from Elizabeth McMullen is a marvelous way to enjoy fall apples.

1 unbaked 9 inch pastry pie shell
6 apples, peeled and sliced thin (Greening, Winesap or Rome Beauties)
1 cup sugar
1/2 teaspoon cinnamon
2 Tablespoons cornstarch
2 Tablespoons lemon juice
1 Tablespoon butter, melted plus 1/3 cup butter
1/2 cup brown sugar
1/2 cup flour
1/2 cup pecans, finely chopped
1/2 teaspoon vanilla

Toss together apples, sugar, cinnamon, cornstarch, lemon juice and 1 Tablespoon melted butter. Pour into pastry.

Combine brown sugar, pecans and flour. Cut in butter and vanilla. Chill in refrigerator. Once firm, form into a ball and roll out between two slices of wax paper, to fit the top of the pie. Remove one piece of wax paper and gently place on top of pie, tapping on pie before removing other piece of wax paper. Bake at 450° for five minutes. Reduce heat to 350° and bake another 45 minutes or until done.

1-1/2 cup sour cream
1/4 cup sugar
1 teaspoon almond flavoring
1/8 teaspoon grated nutmeg

Mix together sour cream, sugar and almond flavoring and pour over the pie while still hot. Sprinkle with nutmeg. Return pie to oven and bake 10 minutes at 400°. Serve hot.

FRESH PEAR TART

This makes a good shallow pie and uses up pears right at the perfect, or over-perfect ripeness. I perfected this while in quarantine in 2020, and it appears in *A Bite of Arkansas*.

1 unbaked 9 inch pastry pie crust
4 fresh pears (combine at least two different pear varietals)
1 stick butter
1 teaspoon vanilla
2 Tablespoons brown sugar

Heat oven to 350°. Blind bake crust for 10 minutes. Let cool.

Slice pears 1/4 inch thick from top to bottom. Arrange half in pie crust with edges overlapping. In a saucepan, combine butter, vanilla and brown sugar. Pour half over bottom layer of pear slices. Arrange remaining pear slices on top. Pour over other half of vanilla butter mixture. Bake for 30 minutes, until pears are tender.

GOOSEBERRY PIE

It's hard to find a gooseberry pie any more, except at the exceptional Gooseberry Handmade Pies in Bentonville, where so many unique and delectable heritage pies can be found (check out their Chocolate Italian Meringue Pie on page 194). This one is out of *Family Cookbook*.

2 unbaked 9 inch pastry pie crusts
4 cups fresh or frozen gooseberries
1 Tablespoon water
1-1/2 cups + 2 teaspoons sugar
1/4 cup all-purpose flour
1/4 teaspoon ground nutmeg
1 tablespoon light cream or milk or egg wash

Roll out one crust to a 12-inch circle. Lay into a 9-inch pie plate. Trim pastry even with rim of pie plate. Set aside.

In a medium saucepan, combine berries and water. Cook over medium-low heat until berries start to burst open, stirring occasionally. Sift together flour, nutmeg and 1-1/2 cups sugar and add to the saucepan. Cook and stir until mixture just begins to bubble.

Spread mixture into the crust. Roll out remaining pastry. Cut slits to allow steam to escape. Place remaining pastry on filling; trim pastry to 1/2 inch beyond edge of pie plate. Fold top pastry under bottom pastry. Brush top crust with cream, milk or egg wash and sprinkle with sugar. Cover the edge of the pie with foil. Bake at 375° for 25 minutes. Remove foil. Bake about 20 minutes more or until top is golden. Cool before serving.

LEMON RASPBERRY TART

This beautiful pastry was created by Vivian McMeekin. It's gorgeous, and being gluten-free just makes it that much more attractive.

Crust
2 cups blanched almond flour
2-1/2 teaspoons coconut flour
4 Tablespoons cold water
1/2 cup sugar
Zest of one lemon
2 teaspoons almond extract
1 teaspoons salt

Curd
1 cup lemon juice
Zest from the lemons you juiced
1/2 cup sugar
2 eggs, beaten
1 Tablespoon coconut oil
3 Tablespoons raspberries

Whipped Cream
4 teaspoons water
1 teaspoon unflavored gelatin
1 cup heavy whipping cream
1/4 cup powdered sugar
1 teaspoon vanilla or orange liqueur

Garnish
Fresh blueberries or raspberries as desired.

Preheat oven to 350° and butter an eight inch tart pan. Combine all crust ingredients in a food processor, and pulse until dough forms a smooth ball. Press dough into buttered tart pan, and bake for 14 minutes until dark golden and puffed. Cool completely.

In a small saucepan, combine all lemon curd ingredients except the raspberries over low heat. Stir constantly for 5-7 minutes, being careful not to let the mixture simmer.

Once mixture is thick and even consistency, remove from heat and transfer to a bowl to cool slightly. Set aside a quarter cup of the curd, then refrigerate the rest, covered, for 30 minutes. Drop the raspberries into the quarter cup of still hot curd and stir until they color it. Strain out seeds and set aside.

Pour yellow lemon curd into crust, and swirl pink curd over the top. Chill tart for at least a an hour before making the whipped cream.

Dissolve gelatin in heated water and set aside. In a large mixing bowl, beat together the whipping cream, powdered sugar and vanilla until soft peaks form, then add softened gelatin. Beat to stiff peaks.

Pipe a ring of this cream around the border of the tart and top with fresh berries. Chill 6 hours or overnight before serving.

The Great Arkansas Pie Book

Fruit Pies

OZARK GRAPE PIE

Lisa Childs shares this recipe for a grape pie from Holly Childs. The dessert has been popular in the Altus and Boston Mountain regions of our state for more than a century.

2 unbaked 9 inch pastry crusts
3 cups Concord or other black grapes
1 cup sugar
3 Tablespoons flour
dash salt
1/2 teaspoon grated lemon rind
3 Tablespoons butter

Slip skins from grapes. Bring pulp to a boil, press through sieve to remove seeds; add skins. Mix flour, sugar, salt and lemon rind and add to grapes. Fill pastry lined pan, dot with butter and cover with top crust (lattice is pretty). Bake at 400° for 30-40 minutes.

OZARK WILD HUCKLEBERRY PIE

Famous for "Good Southern Vittles," Burns Gables was a long-standing waystation along US Highway 71 at the highest point on the route from Fort Smith to Fayetteville. It wasn't just a spot to take in the views but a destination where you could rent a cabin, shop souvenirs and eat in a classic Ozark diner. John and Lavada Burns opened it in 1936. Its name comes from the striking gables atop the original three story lodge. John died in 1947, but Lavada kept on, managing it for the next twenty years. Fire destroyed the oriiginal lodge in 1952. A year later, the more modern restaurant and shop was opened, with the iconic red and green padded chairs and barstools awaiting all comers.

Come they did, for those good Southern meals and, what postcards often described as "luscious pies." In 1963, this recipe for Lavada Burns' Ozark Wild Huckleberry Pie was published in the *New Ford Treasury of Favorite Recipes from Famous Restaurants*, complete with Hot Water Crust.

Crust
1/2 cup lard
1/4 cup hot water
1/4 teaspoon salt
1 and a half cups all-purpose flour

Filling
2-1/2 cups wild huckleberries
1-1/4 cups sugar
3 tablespoons cornstarch
Pinch of salt
1 tablespoon lemon juice

Make the pie crust the day before. Melt the lard and add in the hot water and salt. Mix well. Add in the flour, and knead by hand until the mixture comes together. Form into a disk, wrap with plastic wrap, and chill overnight.

Divide the dough into two halves. Roll out one part to line a 9 inch pie pan. Reserve the other half for the top crust.

Mix the huckleberries, sugar, cornstarch, pinch of salt, and lemon juice in a big mixing bowl. Toss gently to mix all the ingredients. Fill the pie crust with the huckleberry filling, and cover with the top crust. Flute the edges, and create vent holes in the top crust.

Bake in a preheated 450° oven for 10 minutes, then reduce heat to 350° and continue baking until the crust is browned and filling is bubbly, about 35 minutes. Transfer to a baking rack, and let cool. Serve room temperature or cold.

Fruit Pies

PEACH LATTICE PIE

Jan Simrell has been making pies for decades, and is one of the most proficient piemakers I have ever met. She and her husband Ronald moved to Arkansas from Frankfort, Illinois, about 20 miles from Chicago, after her father-in-law, Aaron Simrell, contacted them. He had discovered the Beaver Lake area, and he told her, "Tell your husband to load up the four boys and get them down here - I have found a little bit of heaven." So the couple packed up their four sons - Ronald Junior, Larry, Kurt, and Jody - and moved down to this peninsula on the north shore of the lake.

Jan says "we didn't know what we were getting into. The lake was just four or five years old, and it was so clear and beautiful when it was calm, you could see all the way to the bottom. It's still such a pretty lake with its crystal waters."

Today, Jody manages the property and makes the pizzas at the restaurant, and Jan bakes. The resort has gained fame over the years for the ever-growing fireworks show the family puts on each

The Great Arkansas Pie Book

year. It grows by leaps and bounds, and has become the region's most noted fireworks show, even being cited by *Reader's Digest* in 2022 as the best place to view fireworks in the state of Arkansas..

It's the pies, though, that captured my attention when I went in 2013 to see those fireworks. Grav Weldon and I arrived mid-afternoon, and after touring the munitions that would soon light up the sky with Jody, we sat down for a break with iced tea and slices of Jan's homemade pie. Let me tell you what - the fireworks for me started with the first bite of the succulent peach pie - fresh, pliant peaches with that bit of crunch and the pinkish turn where the pit had been pulled, with just the right amount of spice and splendor to it. The flavor struck me as being one of the best peach pies in Arkansas, and I have been determined to get back ever since to try it again.

That's how in January 2023, while researching this very book, I ended up in Jan and Jody's kitchen on an off-season Monday. While the resort is year-round, the restaurant is only open Thursday through Sunday, Memorial Day to Labor Day, serving burgers, sandwiches, pizzas and salads to guests and visitors. The vintage jukebox plays decades of great pop and country hits. Jody's pizzas get acclaim these days, but during these winter months, the kitchen is oft silent, only opened for special occasions.

Jan has her measurements down pat, rolls her dough with ease, and effortlessly lays each pastry into the pan. She can perfectly flute a pie, knowing well how the press of her finger against the dough makes the perfect semi-circle inch over inch, coming out to a perfect edge every single time. Her crusts are even. She can expertly cut a lattice strip an inch wide or less without a guide, and her hands work so smoothly as she weaves on the lattice over the filling.

Jan and Ron were married for sixty years before he passed in 2016. Their family operation is still strong after all these years, not only because of the fame fireworks have brought to the place, but because of customers who come back as guests again and again. Jody will often grace visitors with his magnificent talent at piano playing, popping out classics from gospel to country to rock, playing the grand piano or a new electronic piano in the meeting room at the other end of the lodge. New developments are always happening - a new pavilion one year, perhaps a smokehouse the next. And Jan's pies continue to bring hungry travelers down windy roads for an afternoon's respite.

The Great Arkansas Pie Book

Fruit Pies

To make Jan's Fresh Peach Pie

3 cups fresh sliced peaches
1 cup sugar
2 Tablespoons butter
1 teaspoon vanilla
1/2 teaspoon almond extract
3/4 cup water
2 Tablespoons cornstarch
2 unbaked 10 inch pastry pie crusts

Mix peaches, sugar, butter and vanilla and 1/2 cup water together and bring to a boil. Simmer until peaches are soft and tender. Do not overcook. Remove from heat.

Add 2 Tablespoons cornstarch mixed with almond extract and remaining water and vanilla. Gently stir into hot peaches. Return to heat. Stir occasionally to thicken. Be careful not to crush peach slices. When thickened, remove from heat.

Prepare the crust. Roll out one crust and put into 10 inch pie plate, leaving about an inch around the edges. Pour hot filling into crust. Roll out second pastry crust and cut into strips for lattice top. Flute around edges with fingers. Lay on the lattice, and then press a fork around the edges to seal the lattice. Bake at 375° in preheated oven for 30 minutes. Reduce to 350° and bake another 30 minutes, until filling is bubbling and crust browned.

PEACH PIE

Nellie B's is always a good bet for satisfying your sweet tooth. I know I can go get a hot lunch and end up taking away an orange or peach roll, a danish or a slice of pie. This recipe for Grandma's Peach Pie Filling comes straight from the source. Check out the pastry dough recipe on page 22.

1 batch Patty's Pastry recipe for double crust pie
6 cups peeled and pitted peaches, sliced
1 teaspoon lemon juice
1 cup sugar
1/4 flour
2 Tablespoons unsalted butter

Mix all ingredients above together except butter, until a thick paste forms around the peach slices. Pour filling into prepared shell, and evenly disperse butter on top of the peaches before placing the top crust.

Finish top crust to your liking, with decorative edges, or sprinkled with crystal sugar.

Cut two slits in the top of the pie for steam, and place in oven at 425° and bake for 35-45 minutes.

PEAR MINCEMEAT PIE FILLING

I remember very few of the recipes my maternal grandmother made. I don't think it's anything other than the fact I didn't really cook with my grandmother. After all, I was just one of 15 grandchildren by the time I started paying attention to the things we'd eat. But I do remember her pear mincemeat. She'd take the hard pears off the scrappy trees out back of the house and process them into dozens of pints of mincemeat every fall.

My mom, when she put together *Cornerstone Cookery*, the cookbook created when she was president of the St. Vincent's Infirmary Employee Council, took down that recipe and recorded it in the book. It's perfect - except it's too large for just one pie.

7 pounds pears, pared and sliced
12 apples, pared and sliced
3 oranges, peeled and sectioned
2 pounds raisins
1-1/2 cups brown sugar
5 cups sugar
1/2 cup white vinegar
1 Tablespoon ground cloves
1 Tablespoon nutmeg
1 Tablespoon cinnamon

Combine all ingredients in large saucepan. Boil for 3 minutes, stirring constantly. Use wooden spoon. Seal in pint or quart jars or freeze.

Fruit Pies

PEAR MINCEMEAT PIE

I worked for several days at The Writers' Colony at Dairy Hollow to squeeze down the recipe for just one pie. And this? It's really good. By simplifying the recipe down to just pears and concentrating on replicating the spices, I managed to come pretty close. I did find that I liked having allspice within the recipe. This is what I came up with.

3 pounds pears, peeled and diced
Rind of one orange, grated
1/2 cup chopped toasted pecans
1 pound raisins
3-1/2 cups sugar
1/3 cup cider vinegar
1/2 teaspoon salt
1-1/2 teaspoons ground nutmeg
1-1/2 teaspoons ground cinnamon
1-1/2 teaspoons ground allspice
1-1/2 teaspoons ground cloves
2 unbaked 9 inch pastry
   pie crusts
1 large egg, lightly beaten

Bring first 11 ingredients to a boil in a large saucepan, stirring often. Reduce to medium and let simmer 30 minutes or until thickened to jam consistency. Allow to cool (or seal in container and refrigerate until ready to use).

Heat oven to 350°. Lay a pie crust into a 9 inch deep dish pie plate. Cut to one inch around plate. Spoon filling into the pie crust. Place second crust over the top, pressing gently to the surface of the mincemeat from the center out. Cut to one inch over all around and tuck under the edge of the first crust. Brush with egg and pierce crust to allow steam to escape. Bake for one hour or until golden brown.

PIANALTO'S PEACH PECAN PIE

The Farmer's Table is an all-green, sustainable restaurant in Fayetteville that is supported by small sustainable family farms in and around the area. Foods are prepared in-season, with an eye towards keeping down food waste and practicing green initiatives. It's also a place where you'll sink your fork into some of the most rustic, locally-sourced and filled pies you'll ever encounter. This recipe from Sidney Pianalto showcases Arkansas pecans, peaches, and honey.

1 cup pecans
1-2 cups sliced peaches
4 Tablespoons butter
3 large eggs
1 cup honey

1/2 cup brown sugar
1/2 teaspoon salt
2 teaspoons vanilla
1 unbaked 9 inch pie crust
   of choice

Brown the butter and let cool for about 5 minutes. Temper butter into eggs with whisk and add honey, brown sugar, salt, and vanilla.

Line pie pan with crust. Slice peaches and place in bottom of pan so that slices cover the bottom but do not overlap. Cover peaches with pecans as evenly as possible. Pour egg mixture over the pecans slowly, distributing as evenly as possible.

Bake at 350° for 30 minutes and then tent with foil and bake another 30 minutes. Center should be almost solid but still have some jiggle. Let set 20-30 minutes and serve.

RED HOT APPLE PIE

I originally made this recipe for a competition a couple of decades back. It's now part of my standard repertoire. Instead of a traditional apple pie, where the apples are stewed or covered in sugar and spices before baking, these are simply dusted with a little salt and sugar and put in a crust before a hot emulsion of cinnamon imperials and butter are poured over. The apples begin their cooking process right then and there, then are finished in the oven. The result is a crispy, candy top crust similar to the outside edge of a candy apple.

3 tart apples, sliced
3 sweet apples, sliced
1 Tablespoon sugar
1/2 teaspoon salt
1/2 pound butter
1-9 ounce bag cinnamon imperials (Red Hots)
1 unbaked 9 inch pastry pie crust
Sugar for dusting, optional

Lay crust into a pie plate. Mix salt and sugar and toss with apple slices. Lay apple slices into pie plate, taking care to set apples so each one has an edge towards the top of the pie.

In a small saucepan, set the butter to melt. Once melted, add all but a small handful of the cinnamon imperials into the butter and stir constantly until the red hots are completely dissolved. The moment the imperials are amalgamated, pour over the apples in the pie shell, making sure to cover the entire top surface of the pie. Fold in any pastry crust edges over the apples before the candy hardens. Dust top of pie with sugar and the rest of the imperials, if desired. Bake at 350° for 30-35 minutes or until the pastry edges are golden. To serve, be sure to crack the crust with the side of the pie server before cutting into the pie and lifting the slice.

RHUBARB PIE

In the 1987 book *The Ozarks Collection* by Billy Joe Tatum and Ann Taylor Packer, a discussion of rhubarb pie brings up its colloquial name. Here in Arkansas, it was usually referred to as pie-plant and rarely by its official name. It was common in gardens in the 19th century, but has lost its popularity here over the past century, perhaps due to milder winters. This recipe cited by Tatum and Packers was found in a Presbyterian cookbook dated to 1901, attributed to one Mrs. C.H.H., called an Old Fashioned Pie-Plant Pie

Select the red stalks of pie-plant early in the spring and cut off where the leaves commence, strip off the outer skin and cut in pieces one-half inch long. Line a pie tin with pie-dough, put a layer of the pie-plant about an inch deep, add one heaping cup of granulated sugar, a sprinkle of salt, and shake over the pie one tablespoon of flour, then cover with top crust with a slit in the center for air bubbles. Next trim the edges of both pieces of dough, crimp together to hold in the juice, and bake in a quick hot oven until done, slightly browned.

Pies made this way are far superior to those made with the pie-plant is first stewed.

Fruit Pies

RHUBARB PIE

Here's a more modern recipe for the dish. Frozen rhubarb can be substituted and be ok. Only use canned rhubarb in a pinch, since it will change the texture and color of the pie.

- 4 cups fresh rhubarb, cut into 1/2 inch pieces
- 1 cup sugar, divided
- 1-3 ounce package strawberry gelatin
- 1 cup water
- 1/4 cup cornstarch
- 1/2 teaspoon cinnamon
- 2-3 drops red food coloring, optional
- 2 unbaked 9 inch pastry crusts

Heat oven to 425°. Bring rhubarb, 1/2 cup sugar and water to a boil in saucepan. Simmer 5 to 10 minutes or until rhubarb is almost tender. Combine remaining 1/2 cup sugar, gelatin, cornstarch and cinnamon in small bowl. Stir into rhubarb and boil one minute. Add food coloring if desired. Spoon into unbaked pie shell. Moisten pastry edge with water.

Cover with top crust. Trim 1/2 inch beyond edge of pie plate. Fold top edge under bottom crust. Flute with fingers or fork. Cut slits or design top crust. Lattice top may be used.

Bake at 425° degrees for 30 minutes or until golden brown. Cool to room temperature before serving.

Variation: CRAN-RASPBERRY PIE

Omit 1 cup rhubarb and strawberry gelatin, and add 1/2 cup frozen or fresh raspberries, 1/2 cup cran-raspberry sauce and one egg.

SPICED BLACKBERRY PIE

Rachel Reynolds is an Ozark folklife expert who has taken a keen interest to Arkansas and its pieways. She came up with a winning entry for the 2022 Arkansas Pie Festival - and has dozens more up her sleeve. This spiced blackberry pie takes advantage of the state's bounty of wild blackberries that grow in abundance all over the state.

Crust
3 cups all-purpose flour
1 Tablespoon cornstarch
2 Tablespoons sugar
1-1/2 teaspoons salt
1-1/2 sticks of salted butter
1/4 cup of lard
3/4 cup 2% milk
1 Tablespoon apple cider vinegar

Filling
5-1/3 cups fresh blackberries
1 stick (1/4 pound) salted butter
1 cup light brown sugar
1 teaspoon cinnamon
2 teaspoons ground ginger
3 Tablespoons all-purpose flour

Egg white for egg wash (optional)
Raw sugar to dust crust

Fruit Pies

Preheat oven to 350°.

To make crust, add apple cider vinegar to milk and set aside. Mix flour, cornstarch, sugar, and salt in a large bowl. Cut chilled butter and lard into small pieces and add to dry mix. Cut in with a pastry cutter until small beads form. Add milk mixture and stir until mixed in. Form two balls of dough, working as little as possible. Roll out one ball and place in pie plate (I use a cast iron pie plate for this one). Reserve other ball, cover to keep moist.

Melt butter over low heat in a thick sauce pan. Add sugar and stir until melted. Add washed berries. Add spices. Add flour and stir until all combined. Pour in prepared crust.

Roll out other dough ball for top crust. Place across top. Brush egg white over entire top crust and edges. Sprinkle sugar all over the crust.

Bake until light golden brown, about an hour.

STRAWBERRY PIE

During Arkansas's splendid strawberry season, two dishes sprout across the land - legendary strawberry shortcakes, like those offered at The Bulldog Restaurant in Bald Knob and Trio's in Little Rock - and fresh strawberry pies. The latter come in an array, from strawberry cream to strawberry cream cheese, but it is the fresh strawberry pie that draws the most oohs and ahhs. While pulling that recipe from any of our celebrated local operations proved for naught, I do have in my collection a handwritten recipe from the old Jacksonville Shoney's, where (before it closed several years back) strawberry pie was a popular favorite.

1 cup water
1 cup granulated sugar
3 Tablespoons cornstarch
6 Tablespoons strawberry Jell-O

1 pound whole strawberries, with stem removed
1 baked 9 inch deep-dish pastry crust or graham cracker crust

Stir sugar, cornstarch, and water together in a medium-sized pot over medium heat. Cook stirring occasionally, until the glaze coats the back of a spoon. Add Jell-O to the glaze and stir to combine.

Place drained whole fresh strawberries into pie shell. Pour cooked mixture over berries. Chill at least two hours. Top with whipped cream or whipped topping if desired.

NUT PIES

BOURBON CHOCOLATE CHUNK PECAN PIE

The decadent Bourbon Chocolate Chunk Pecan pie offered by Chef Jerrmy Gawthrop at the former Greenhouse Grille in Fayetteville. is one of my favorite pies, ever. The farm-to-fork restaurant was well known for its use of hyper-local produce, meats and fungi – including the magnificent shiitake fries with magic catsup.

6 medium eggs
2 cups brown rice syrup
  or corn syrup
2 cups brown sugar
1/3 cup bourbon (Jack Daniels)

4 ounces semi-sweet
  chocolate chunks
2 baked 9 inch pastry pie crusts
2 and 2/3 cups toasted pecans

Beat eggs until smooth. Slowly add syrup and brown sugar. Pour in bourbon and mix thoroughly. Place chocolate chunks across bottom of pie shells. Pour batter over the chocolate. Top with pecans. Place on sheet pan and bake in preheated 350° oven for 45 to 50 minutes or until center is firm. Makes two pies.

Nut Pies

BOURBON CHOCOLATE PECAN PIE

DeVito's Restaurant, the long-running eatery and trout farm, has been serving up great fish dinners with all the accoutrements for decades. After a repast of trout pâté, trout Italiano and trout fingers, it may be hard to save room for a piece of this decadent pie. I'd suggest getting it to go - or attempting this DeVito family recipe.

- 1 homemade vegetable shortening pie crust (see page 24)
- 4 large eggs
- 1 cup light corn syrup
- 6 Tablespoons butter
- 1/2 cup sugar
- 3 tablespoons bourbon
- 1/4 cup firmly packed light brown sugar
- 1 teaspoon all-purpose flour
- 1 teaspoon vanilla extract
- 1 cup coarsely chopped pecans
- 1 cup (6 ounces) semi-sweet chocolate chips

Fit pie crust into a 9-inch pie plate. Fold edges under and crimp. Whisk together eggs and next seven ingredients until mixture is smooth. Stir in pecans and morsels. Pour into pie crust. Bake on lowest rack at 350° degrees for one hour or until set.

BLACK WALNUT PIE

Black walnut trees can be found growing all over Arkansas. During harvest season, you'll notice large tennis ball sized green spheres on trees. These shield a hard nut that's worth cracking and eating. The nuts have a stronger flavor than typical walnuts, which makes them great for imparting a nutty flavor in most foods. Pairing them with sorghum molasses is a natural touch.

- 1 unbaked 9 inch pastry pie crust
- 1 cup black walnuts, chopped
- 1/4 cup butter, melted
- 1/2 cup brown rice syrup
- 1/2 cup sorghum molasses
- 3 eggs, beaten
- 1/2 teaspoon vanilla

Fit crust to pie plate. Spread the chopped walnuts over the bottom of the pie shell and set aside.

Blend the butter and syrups with eggs and vanilla. Pour the mixture over the nuts and place the pie in a pre-heated 425° oven for 15 minutes. Reduce the heat to 350° and continue baking for 25 minutes or until top cracks slightly. Cool thoroughly before cutting.

Nut Pies

BUTTERMILK PECAN PIE

Ellen Wood's recipe from the 2014 *Van Buren County Extension Homemakers Council's Recipes* shows a beautiful alternate to the traditional Karo nut pie. To guild the lily, add sugar glazed pecan halves to the top of the pie before baking. Be sure to make a foil tent for your pie.

1 unbaked pastry pie crust
1 stick butter, melted
1 and 1/2 cup sugar
1 cup buttermilk
1/4 cup all purpose flour

3 eggs
1 teaspoon vanilla
1/2 teaspoon salt
1 cup glazed pecans, crushed
1 cup glazed pecans halves *(opt.)*

Mix together butter, sugar, buttermilk and flour. Add eggs, vanilla, and salt. Pour into crust set into prepared 10 inch or deep dish 9 inch pie plate. Drop crushed pecans over top of mixture (they will likely sink). Arrange pecan halves around edge of pie. Tent pie with foil and bake at 350° for 50 minute, removing foil the last 10 minutes.

BROWN SUGAR PECAN PIE

For those who eschew corn syrup, this version of the traditional Karo nut pie is a blessing. Plus, the vanilla flavor really shines.

2 eggs, beaten
2 sticks (1/2 pound) butter, melted
1 cup light brown sugar
1/4 cup sugar
1 teaspoon vanilla
1 Tablespoon all-purpose flour
1 cup chopped pecans
1/2 cup pecan halves
1 unbaked 9 inch pastry pie crust

Heat oven to 350°. Beat the heck out of the eggs. Pour in the melted butter, both sugars and the vanilla and incorporate thoroughly. Shake chopped pecans with all-purpose flour and add to the mix.

Pour into pie shell. Top with pecan halves. Bake for 45 minutes or until inserted toothpick comes out clean.

CARAMEL NUT PIE

I have so many squirreled away recipes here and there for our greatest pie places. Sue's Pie Shop certainly fit the bill. There's not a pie from her place I didn't love. This one in particular became a favorite.

Filling
3/4 cup sugar
1/4 cup all-purpose flour
1/4 cup unsweetened cocoa
1/4 teaspoon salt
2 cups milk
2 egg yolks
1 tablespoon butter
1 teaspoon vanilla extract
Whipped cream, optional

Topping
1 egg yolk
1/4 cup granulated sugar
2-1/2 tablespoons milk
1/4 teaspoon vanilla extract
2 tablespoons butter
1/4 cup chopped pecans

1 baked 9 inch pastry pie crust

In a medium saucepan, mix sugar, flour, cocoa and salt. Add milk and cook over medium heat until mixture thickens and comes to a boil. Add a little hot filling to the beaten egg yolks to temper, then add egg yolk mixture to saucepan. Cook until it returns to a full boil. Remove from heat, stir in butter and vanilla; cool. Pour into pre-baked pie shell.

Beat egg yolk in small saucepan. Gradually add sugar, mixing well. Add in milk, vanilla and butter. Cook over medium heat until thick. Cool. Stir in pecans and spread over pie filling. Refrigerate. Garnish with whipped cream, if desired.

Nut Pies

NANA DEANE'S COCONUT PECAN PIE

Ray's Dairy Maid once stood alongside US Highway 49 in the Barton community, to the west of Helena-West Helena. There, Nana Deane Cavette ran the shop and made the pies. Her coconut pecan pie became famous when it was first featured on Alton Brown's *Feasting on Asphalt: River Road Run* on Food Network. The recipe appears in the book that came out with the series - and in my first book, *Arkansas Pie: A Delicious Slice of The Natural State*.

10.5 ounces granulated sugar
3 large whole eggs
2 ounces unsalted butter, melted
4 ounces buttermilk
1 tablespoon all-purpose flour
1 teaspoon vanilla extract

Pinch salt
3 ounces chopped pecans
 (approximately 3/4 cup)
3 ounces sweetened coconut
 flakes
1 unbaked 9-inch pastry pie crust

Preheat oven to 350°. In a large mixing bowl, combine the sugar, eggs, melted butter, buttermilk, coconut, pecans, flour, vanilla and salt. Pour into pie crust. Bake for 45 minutes or until the pie is golden brown and the center is barely set. Cool for 40-45 minutes before serving.

GERMAN CHOCOLATE PECAN PIE

Mandi Palmer makes pies for Mack's Fish House in Heber Springs. She also has a spot called Sweet Treats by Mandi. This gorgeous pie is one of her best sellers.

- 1 cup white sugar
- 1 cup dark Karo corn syrup
- 1 Tablespoons vanilla extract
- 3 Tablespoons melted salted butter
- 3 eggs
- 1/2 cup coconut
- 1/2 cup semi-sweet chocolate chips
- 3/4 cup chopped pecans
- 1 deep dish pastry pie crust

In a medium bowl mix sugar, corn syrup, eggs, vanilla and butter.

Put the coconut, chocolate chips and pecans in the bottom of a deep dish pie crust. Pour the egg and sugar mixture over. Let sit a few minutes so everything settles. Add pie to a 345° oven for 35-45 minutes. Best served warm with a scoop of ice cream.

HICKORY NUT PIE

"Hickernuts," as I've heard all my life, are hard as wood and hurt like hell when they're pitched at you. Despite this, I do love their flavor. But man, they're a pain in the butt to get that meat out of their shells. Regardless, you get it out, you have the beginning of a truly remarkable pie that will have you thinking of fall.

Crust
- 1.5 cups all-purpose flour
- 1/2 cup vegetable shortening
- 1 teaspoon sugar
- 1/2 teaspoon salt
- 1/4 teaspoon nutmeg
- About 1/2 cup cold water

Filling
- 2 cups hickory nut pieces
- 3 large eggs
- 1/2 cup light brown sugar
- 3/4 cup sorghum molasses
- 3 Tablespoons butter
- 2 Tablespoons bourbon
- 1 teaspoon vanilla extract
- 1/4 teaspoon salt

Mix flour, shortening, sugar, nutmeg and salt together with a fork or a pastry blender until very crumbly. Add as much cold water as needed until the dough just holds together.

Form the dough into a ball and cover with plastic wrap. Refrigerate for at least an hour.

Roll the dough gently on a floured surface at least two inches larger than the pie pan. Lay into pan and press in with knuckles to create a rugged surface.

Preheat oven to 375°. Line crust with foil and fill with dried beans or pie weights. Blind bake for 30 minutes. Remove the foil and weights and allow the crust to cool.

Beat together eggs and brown sugar in a medium bowl. Beat in the sorghum. Add butter, bourbon, vanilla, and salt; beat until blended. Stir in nuts. Pour into crust. Return to the oven and bake 25 minutes or until the center is fully set. Allow to cool completely. Serve warm and topped with sweetened whipped cream, if desired.

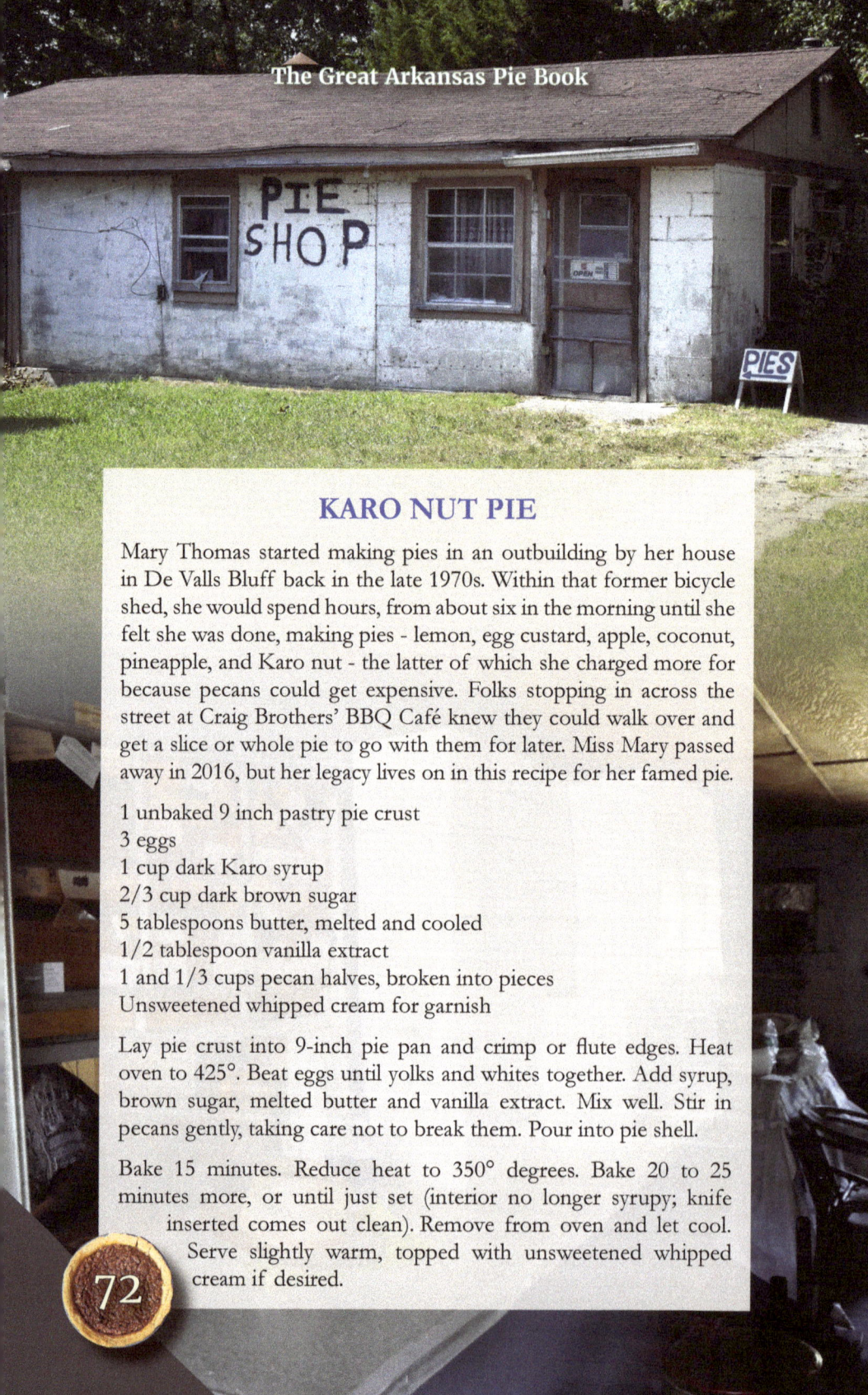

KARO NUT PIE

Mary Thomas started making pies in an outbuilding by her house in De Valls Bluff back in the late 1970s. Within that former bicycle shed, she would spend hours, from about six in the morning until she felt she was done, making pies - lemon, egg custard, apple, coconut, pineapple, and Karo nut - the latter of which she charged more for because pecans could get expensive. Folks stopping in across the street at Craig Brothers' BBQ Café knew they could walk over and get a slice or whole pie to go with them for later. Miss Mary passed away in 2016, but her legacy lives on in this recipe for her famed pie.

1 unbaked 9 inch pastry pie crust
3 eggs
1 cup dark Karo syrup
2/3 cup dark brown sugar
5 tablespoons butter, melted and cooled
1/2 tablespoon vanilla extract
1 and 1/3 cups pecan halves, broken into pieces
Unsweetened whipped cream for garnish

Lay pie crust into 9-inch pie pan and crimp or flute edges. Heat oven to 425°. Beat eggs until yolks and whites together. Add syrup, brown sugar, melted butter and vanilla extract. Mix well. Stir in pecans gently, taking care not to break them. Pour into pie shell.

Bake 15 minutes. Reduce heat to 350° degrees. Bake 20 to 25 minutes more, or until just set (interior no longer syrupy; knife inserted comes out clean). Remove from oven and let cool. Serve slightly warm, topped with unsweetened whipped cream if desired.

Nut Pies

KENTUCKY DERBY PIE

In 2006, Patti Stobaugh opened PattiCakes Bakery, initially an extension of the famous Stoby's Restaurant, where the popular rolls and pies were made. It's grown since into a bustling, bursting business with two Conway outlets, with a reputation for excellent sandwiches and lunches, take-and-bakes, croissants, cookies, macarons and pies. While we chatted all about possum pie in the 2018 documentary *Make Room for Pie*, this pie right here is another wonderful favorite.

4 large eggs
1 cup light corn syrup
1/2 cup packed brown sugar
1/4 teaspoon salt
1/2 teaspoon vanilla
2 Tablespoons bourbon
1 Tablespoon butter
1 cup chopped pecans
1/2 cup chocolate chips
1 unbaked 9 inch pastry pie shell

Put chopped pecans and chocolate chips in unbaked pie shell. Beat eggs. Add remaining ingredients to eggs and mix well. Pour into pie shell. Bake at 350° for 45 minutes or until set

LEMON PECAN PIE

Ruby Pierce Jones spent more than seven decades of her life cooking for other people - first her family, then as the cook at Central Grill in Pine Bluff in the 1930s and 1940s, then at Jones Café in Noble Lake starting in 1948. In 1988, her collection of recipes was published as *The Best of Ruby Jones*, a widely distributed cookbook.

Crust

2 cups all-purpose flour
1 teaspoon sugar
1/2 teaspoon salt
3/8 teaspoon baking powder
1/4 cup milk
7 Tablespoons olive oil

Filling

5 tablespoons salted butter
4 large *or* 3 extra-large eggs
1 and 1/4 cups granulated sugar
3/4 cup pecan halves or pieces
1/2 lemon
1 teaspoon lemon extract
pinch salt

Heat oven to 300° For the crust, whisk the flour, sugar, salt and baking powder in a 9-inch pie dish. Whisk the milk and olive oil in a measuring cup and add the liquid to the pie dish. Toss with a fork to blend. Press the dough evenly into the bottom and up the sides of the pie dish to form a crust. Crimp the edges with two fingers.

For the filling, melt the butter in a small pan on the stove over medium-high heat. While it's melting, crack the eggs into a small mixing bowl. Add the sugar and pecans to the bowl. Add the melted butter to the egg mixture. Squeeze in the juice from the half a lemon. Add the lemon extract and salt. Use a fork to stir until combined. Pour the filling into the unbaked pie crust.

Bake the pie for 50-52 minutes, until top is set and starting to brown. Let the pie cool on a wire rack. Then refrigerate until set. Serve chilled. Garnish with extra pecans, if desired. Store leftovers in the refrigerator for up to five days.

Nut Pies

NUTTY CHIP PIE

The Good Cooks Cook Book by the Garland County Extension Homemakers' Council is packed with a lot of great pie recipes, including this chocolate ship and nut pie from Ann Vick of LaCasa EHC.

1 stick butter, melted
1 cup sugar
1/2 cup sifted flour
2 eggs, slightly beaten
1 teaspoon vanilla
3/4 cup chocolate chips
1 cup chopped nuts (English walnuts or pecans)
1 unbaked 9 inch pastry pie crust

Mix the first seven ingredients together. Pour into pie shell. Bake at 350° for 30-35 minutes. If center is not firm, bake a little longer. Serve warm. Top with whipped cream if desired.

PECAN PIE

For a simple yet trustworthy pecan pie, look no further than this recipe from the Oark General Store.

1 unbaked 9 inch pastry pie crust
3 eggs, well beaten
1 teaspoon vanilla
1 cup pecans
1 cup brown sugar
1/4 cup butter
1 cup corn syrup

Place pecans across bottom of pie shell. Mix all other ingredients together and pour over pecans. Bake in 350° oven for approximately 45 minutes or until center is slightly jiggly.

Nut Pies

PECAN PIE

This version from Alma Fletcher appears in *Feed My Sheep* by Second Baptist Church in 1987.

1 cup chopped pecans
1 cup corn syrup
1/2 cup sugar
3 eggs, well beaten
1/2 teaspoon salt
3 Tablespoons butter
1 teaspoon vanilla
1 partly baked 8 inch pastry pie crust

Beat eggs. Add remaining ingredients. Bake at 325° for 45 minutes. The nuts will float to the top while baking.

TRUE SOUTH PECAN PIE

My friend Kathie Dawn Johnson of Fort Smith shares this version of the classic pecan pie, which first appeared in *Another Slice of Arkansas Pie*.

1 unbaked 9 inch pie crust
1-1/2 cups chopped pecans
  or pecan halves
3 eggs, beaten
1/2 cup sugar

3 Tablespoons butter, melted
1 cup dark corn syrup
  or 1/2 cup light & 1/2 cup dark
1/4 teaspoon ground cinnamon
1 teaspoon vanilla extract

Preheat oven to 350°. Place pan with pie crust on a baking sheet while preparing the filling.

In medium bowl, whisk together beaten eggs, sugar, melted butter, corn syrup, ground cinnamon and vanilla thoroughly. Put pecans evenly into the bottom of your pie crust. Pour filling slowly on top of the pecans. Bake about 45-50 minutes. After 20 minutes, add a pie shield or aluminum foil over crust to keep it from getting too brown.

You know it is done when the middle of the pie is "set" and not jiggling like gelatin, and the center is a bit puffy. Allow to cool to room temperature before storing covered in refrigerator.

PECAN PIE x 10

Little Rock businessman Ed Moore and Chef Paul Bash of the famed Restaurant Jacques et Suzanne's opened The Purple Cow Restaurant on Cantrell Road in Little Rock back in 1989. The eatery pays homage to the great classic diners of the 1950s, with burgers, shakes, and slices of pie amongst the offerings. Chef Todd Gold shared with me this bulk recipe to make ten of those pies at a time!

7 cups sugar
33 whole eggs, slightly beaten
4 cups dark Karo syrup
5 cup light Karo syrup
1/4 cup molasses
1 pound brown sugar

2 teaspoons salt
1 pound butter, melted
1/4 cup real vanilla
4 pounds pecan pieces
10 unbaked 9 inch pastry
  pie crusts

Preheat oven to 400°. Mix all ingredients together, then pour into pie crusts. Use two full sheet pans, 5 pies on each. Place in oven and reduce oven to 350°. Bake for 20 minutes at 350°. Switch pans around, from front to back and top to bottom. Bake for 20 minutes at 300°. Then bake at 250° for 10 minutes more. Remove from oven and let stand till completely cooled.

Nut Pies

PECAN PIE

Why so many pecan pie recipes? Because this amazing nut, indigenous to Arkansas, appears everywhere. It's a stunningly good protein and so tasty. This version is from Blue Cake Honey Pies in Little Rock.

- 4 egg yolks
- 1/3 cup dark corn syrup
- 1/2 cup light brown sugar
- 4 Tablespoons melted butter
- 1/4 cup heavy cream
- pinch kosher salt
- 1 teaspoon vanilla extract
- 1-1/4 cups pecan halves
- 1 All-Butter Pie Crust (see page 21)

Heat oven to 350°. Melt butter. Mix with corn syrup, sugar and salt.

Whisk egg yolks, heavy cream and vanilla until smooth. Add to sugar mixture and whisk until smooth. If mixture has any lumps, strain to remove.

Using par-baked pie shells for the flakiest crust, portion pecan halves into crusts and add filling (as full as possible).

Bake until filling is set and pie just begins to puff up, to an internal temp of 192°. Do not overbake, or filling will "scramble."

PECAN PIE

Chef Matthew McClure honed his craft through years at Little Rock's famed Capital Hotel and the prestigious The Hive at 21c in Bentonville. The seven-times James Beard Award nominated chef has moved on to endeavors outside the state, but shares his extraordinary pecan pie recipe here. This makes multiple pies.

Filling
2 cups corn syrup
2 cups brown sugar
1 cup heavy cream
1/2 cup molasses
6 eggs yolks
7.75 grams all purpose flour
1/2 Tablespoon vanilla paste
1 teaspoon salt
1 stick butter, cubed

Short dough crust
680g (1 pound, 8 ounces) sugar
1,924g (4 pounds, 4 ounces) bread flour
2 Tablespoons salt
1585g (3 pounds, 8 ounces) butter
4 eggs
4 teaspoons vanilla

Pecans for each portion (see below)

Combine all ingredients in standing mixer bowl. Mix with paddle attachment until combined and dough is smooth. Refrigerate until firm.

Portion and roll dough for tart pans: rectangles should measure 2" bigger than tart pans and be 1/4 inch thick. Layer between pieces of parchment paper and freezing until ready to use.

Thaw frozen pre-shaped dough and gently press into tart pans, carefully trim tops of dough. Place in freezer until firm.

Line each pie plate with parchment paper, and fill with pie weights. Bake at 375°, low fan, for 15-20 minutes, or until edges of crust are lightly golden.

Remove pie weights and parchment, decrease temperature to 325° and cook for another 5-10 minutes, or until bottom of crust is set and beginning to turn golden.

Nut Pies

In a large pot, combine corn syrup, brown sugar, heavy cream, and molasses and bring to a boil.

Meanwhile, whisk together yolks, flour, vanilla, and salt. Temper with sugar mixture and then whisk together.

Pour filling through a chinoise over a hotel pan with the butter. Whisk together until butter is melted. Chill until completely cool.

To bake - use half a pound of pecans for each 20 ounces filling. Portion into pre-baked pie shells. Bake at 250°, low fan, for 40-50 minutes. Rotate the pans after the first 20 minutes.

When finished, pies will be almost completely set with only a slight jiggle in the center.

Cool completely before removing from pans and slicing into portions.

MISS BETTY'S PECAN PIE

Cheryl DeLong is a personal chef who's gained a great reputation in central Arkansas for creating ready-to-serve meals for families. She always has a fabulous recipe for anything you can dream up. She shares: "The tasty variation on a classic is named for my mother, Mrs. Elizabeth Smith who taught me how to cook and is in no small way the reason I can pursue my passion as well as use my talent. I share it now because I want it to continue on and please other families as much as it always has mine."

3 eggs
1/2 cup sugar
1/2 cup light brown sugar
1/2 cup light Karo syrup
1/2 cup dark Karo Syrup
1 teaspoon vanilla extract
1/2 teaspoon kosher salt
2 Tablespoons unsalted butter, melted
1 and a half cup pecan pieces
1 unbaked 9 inch pastry pie crust

Place all ingredients into a medium sized mixing bowl using a rubber spatula to incorporate. Work them together until the sugar is no longer a prominent chunk; the mixture should be smooth save the pecan pieces. Then simply pour into your pre-made pie shell. Bake at 350° for approximately 30 minutes, using the prepared pie shell recipe that follows.

This pie will look darker and firmer than most store-bought pies as the result of mixing sugars and syrups. If the thought of adding salt to the pie bothers you, use salted butter!

Flaky All Butter Pie Crust
2 and a 1/2 cups all purpose flour
   (reserve 1/2 cup for rolling out)
1 teaspoon kosher salt
1 Tablespoon sugar
1/3 cup ice water
1 cup butter, cold, cut into 1/2 Tablespoon chunks

Using a medium sized mixing bowl combine flour, salt and sugar with a whisk or fork. Add butter to the dry mix, then begin to slowly work the dough using your hands and ergo your body

Nut Pies

heat to combine. Ideally the butter and flour should come to pea sized balls. Slowly add the water. Keep the mixture cool by working expediently.

Once your dough becomes supple to the touch with no more sandy bits of flour, make into a ball. Wrap tightly in plastic wrap then place in the fridge to allow to rest 20 to 30 minutes.

Dust your board with the reserved flour, then place your chilled dough in the center. With a rolling pin, roll out the dough to 1/2 inch thickness. Turn the dough between passes; that way the butter will be evenly spread into the dough.

Once desired thickness, drape over chosen dish, dock (poke holes with fork) the dough, and make the edges using the same fork or crimp using your fingers.

Refrigerate the dough another 20-30 minutes before using to make pecan pie. Blind baking isn't necessary for pecan pie but can be done for the sake of a custard that cooks quicker.

The Great Arkansas Pie Book

PECAN TARTS

This perfect recipe makes the perfect pecan tart - just use the crust you prefer. The recipe from Wanda Henson appears in the 2007 cookbook *Barton Memories*.

- 1 cup ground or finely chopped pecans
- 2 eggs
- 1/4 cup light Karo syrup
- 1 cup light brown sugar
- 1 Tablespoon vanilla
- 1/2 cup butter
- 12 pecan halves for garnish
- 12 unbaked pastry pie tart shells

Cream butter. Add brown sugar, eggs, Karo syrup, vanilla and nuts. Fill 12 unbaked tart shells. Place pecan half on top of each. Bake at 325° for 25-30 minutes.

CREAM PIES

Cream, Cream Cheese and Icebox

ALLIGATOR PIE

This amusing name for a lime juice pie was conjured by Heather Petzak, the daughter of Toni Ladd Petzak. The loose page from a cookbook was found tucked into another cookbook. I include it here for the simple recipe and amusing name.

1 large carton Cool Whip
1 can Eagle Brand condensed milk
2-3 drops green food coloring
1 can thawed lime juice
1 prepared graham cracker crust

Mix first four ingredients well. Pour into pie crust. Refrigerate 2-3 hours until firm.

BANOFEE PIE

My friend Amanda Moore shares this recipe from her friend who lives part time in both Ireland and the United States. It's similar to the only banofee pie you'll find regularly on any Arkansas restaurant menu, that of the restaurant at Whispering Woods up near Norfolk. It's a magnificent toffee dream.

Base
10 ounces graham crackers
 (2 sleeves from a box)
5 ounces salted butter

Toffee Filling
4 ounces (1 stick) butter
3/4 cups brown sugar
1 and a 1/2 cups sweetened
 condensed milk
1 teaspoon pure vanilla extract
7/8 teaspoon sea salt pinch

Banana and Cream Topping
3 small bananas
 or 2 medium bananas
1 and a 1/4 cups heavy cream
2 teaspoons powdered sugar
2 ounces milk or dark chocolate
 melted for decorative finish
 (or cocoa powder to dust the top)

Line an 8-inch round springform cake pan with parchment paper and grease the sides. Crush graham cracker into crumbs using a food processor, or place in a ziptop bag and crush with a rolling pin. Place the crumbs in a bowl.

Cream Pies

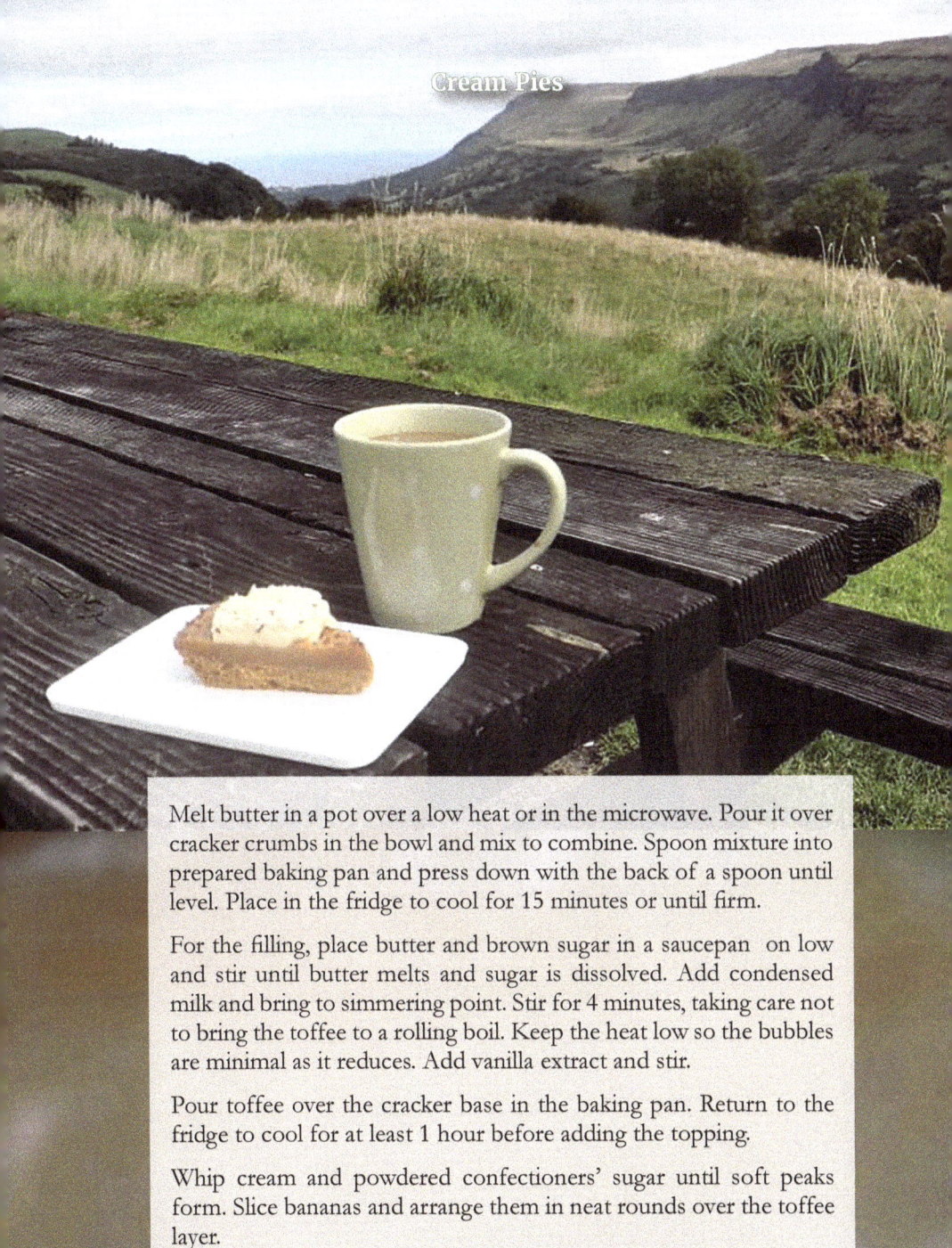

Melt butter in a pot over a low heat or in the microwave. Pour it over cracker crumbs in the bowl and mix to combine. Spoon mixture into prepared baking pan and press down with the back of a spoon until level. Place in the fridge to cool for 15 minutes or until firm.

For the filling, place butter and brown sugar in a saucepan on low and stir until butter melts and sugar is dissolved. Add condensed milk and bring to simmering point. Stir for 4 minutes, taking care not to bring the toffee to a rolling boil. Keep the heat low so the bubbles are minimal as it reduces. Add vanilla extract and stir.

Pour toffee over the cracker base in the baking pan. Return to the fridge to cool for at least 1 hour before adding the topping.

Whip cream and powdered confectioners' sugar until soft peaks form. Slice bananas and arrange them in neat rounds over the toffee layer.

Top with cream and level with the back of a spoon. Allow to cool in the fridge before serving.

To serve, remove from the baking pan. Decorate with zig zags of melted chocolate on top.

BANANA PUDDING PIE

Jackson's Cookie Company once sat in downtown North Little Rock, creating so many excellent cookies and flavoring the air with sweetness. Its most famous products were the lemon flavored Jackson Jumble and the classic Jackson's Vanilla Wafer - the latter a crisp, light and perfect example of what a vanilla wafer should be.

This pie is meant for those wafers. Sadly, any comparison just isn't quite right. Though Ferrero Roche, who bought the rights to the cookie recipe, discontinued it at the end of 2022, I hold out hope it'll sell that recipe to another company so these cookies can return. Until then, use your next best generic vanilla wafer. I suggest toasting your wafers and letting them cool before proceeding with this recipe.

1 - 11 ounce package vanilla wafers
1 stick butter
4-5 bananas, sliced
3 cups cold milk
2 - 3.4 ounce packages. vanilla pudding
1 cup heavy whipping cream

Crush 1 cup of the vanilla wafers. Melt butter, combine with crushed wafers and place in bottom of pie pan.

Mix together pudding powder and cold milk. Reserve 1/3 of mix. Alternate layers of pudding, cookies and bananas. Fold remaining 1/3 of pudding into well beaten heavy whipping cream and pile on top. Chill for 30 minutes before serving.

Cream Pies

BANANA RUM PIE

When I shared this pie at The Writers' Colony at Dairy Hollow, my slices came with the warning of a very boozy pie experience. Indeed, just making this pie was enough to make my mouth wince at the sheer onslaught of rum - particularly the clear rum I'd chosen, rather than the spiced rum I suspect was originally intended. No matter - it was quickly consumed, a nice sweet, cold yet warming delight on a February evening. Somehow, it was better with the rum itself than the rum flavoring, so I've included both directions here.

This recipe is from Emily Alexander, originally published in 1980 in the Benton Junior Auxiliary's *Calico Cupboards* cookbook.

- 1 - 3.75 ounce package instant vanilla pudding mix
- 1 envelope unflavored gelatin
- 2 and 1/4 cups milk
- 1 package fluffy white frosting mix prepared to directions *or* 1 tub fluffy white frosting
- 1.5 teaspoons rum flavoring *or* 1 Tablespoon rum
- 1/8 teaspoon salt
- 1/8 teaspoon nutmeg
- 3 bananas
- 1 baked 9 inch pastry pie shell

In medium saucepan, combine pudding mix, gelatin and milk, Cook according to pudding mix directions. Remove from heat, cover with wax paper and set aside.

Stir rum or rum flavoring, salt, and nutmeg into frosting. Fold hot pudding into frosting mix. Slice one and a half bananas into the pastry shell. Top with half the filling. Repeat. Chill 3-4 hours before serving.

BLUEBERRY BANANA CREAM PIE

My friend Keith Dixon makes this pie, from a recipe he learned from his mom. It first appeared in *Another Slice of Arkansas Pie.*

1 large prepared graham cracker crust in 8 or 9 inch pie pan
2 large bananas, peeled and sliced
1 cup powdered sugar
1/2 container whipped topping
1-8 ounce block cream cheese
1 teaspoon vanilla (optional)
1 can blueberry pie filling
1 can blueberries (optional)

Line bottom of crust with bananas. Blend together cream cheese, vanilla, sugar, and whipped topping. Place the cream cheese mixture on top of bananas. If using canned blueberries, drain well and stir into blueberry filling. Place the blueberry filling on top of the cream cheese mixture. Chill for two hours before serving.

BLUEBERRY CREAM PIE

Another winner from the venerable Sue's Pie Shop that once served Little Rock, this one is built on a handmade custard.

Filling
2/3 cup sugar
1/4 cup flour
1/4 teaspoon salt
2 cups milk
2 egg yolks
1 Tablespoon butter
1 teaspoon vanilla
1 baked 9 inch pastry pie shell

Topping
1 can blueberries
1/3 cup sugar
2 Tablespoons flour
1/4 teaspoon salt
1 Tablespoon butter

For filling: mix sugar, flour and salt together in a saucepan. Add milk and cook over medium heat until thickened and it comes to a full boil. Temper beaten egg yolks, then add egg mixture to the hot liquid. Continue cooking until it again comes to a full boil. Remove from heat, add butter and vanilla. Cool, then spread into baked pie shell. Chill.

For the blueberry topping, cook blueberries, sugar, flour and salt until thick. When it starts to boil, remove from heat. Stir in butter and cool. Spread over cream filling and chill to serve. Garnish with whipped cream and maraschino cherries or whole blueberries.

Cream Pies

BLUEBERRY TORTE

Liza Ashley, who served as cook at the Arkansas Governor's Mansion for three decades, would often make this dish as dessert for dinner parties during David Pryor's administration in the latter half of the 1970s. I like to make this in advance and freeze it; it defrosts overnight and is ready to go to whatever potluck I attend.

1 cup flour
1/2 cup chopped pecans
1/4 cup brown sugar
1/2 cup butter
1-8 ounce package cream cheese

1 cup powdered sugar
1 teaspoon vanilla
2 envelopes Dream Whip
1 cup milk
1 can blueberry pie filling

Mix flour, pecans, brown sugar and butter together. Press into bottom of 9x13" casserole dish or two 9" pie plates. Bake at 400° for 15 minutes or until done.

Mix cream cheese, sugar and vanilla together. Beat Dream Whip with milk and mix into cream cheese blend. Pour into crust. Spread filling over the top. Cover. Chill at least eight hours or overnight.

CARAMEL PECAN CREAM CHEESE PIE

When it came time to put together the documentary *Make Room for Pie* for Arkansas PBS, Larry Foley had just one suggestion. He felt very strongly that The Wooden Spoon in Gentry should be the final restaurant we shared in the film, and he was right. Cam and Jane Klassen's family venture, an eatery that started out as a sandwich shop inside the Spavinaw Stove Works across the street, is now a must-stop for lunchgoers in Arkansas's far northwest corner. The edifice, a pre-1870 horse barn original located on a Michigan farm, was brought down and reassembled for the perfect showcase for the good home cooking the Klassens brought to the table.

In 2021, the Klassens retired, selling the restaurant to Justin and Emily Allen. The menu remains almost exactly the same, down to the lovely varieties of pie available at the front counter and in the case in the dining room. This one is my favorite.

Cream pie base

4 ounces cream cheese
2/3 cup powdered sugar
2 teaspoons vanilla
2 teaspoons instant vanilla pudding
1-1/2 cup heavy whipping cream
1 baked 9 inch pastry pie crust

Beat cream cheese, powdered sugar, vanilla, and instant pudding together well. Whip cream, then fold into cream cheese mixture. Place in bottom of pastry pie crust, cover with topping, drizzle with caramel sauce. Great with more whipped cream on top.

(This filling can also be used to make strawberry cream cheese, fresh peach cream cheese, fresh raspberry cream cheese, blueberry cream cheese and cherry cream cheese pies)

Cream Pies

Caramel pecan cream cheese pie topping

1 cup chopped pecans
1 cup flaked coconut
1/4 cup melted margarine

Combine and bake at 350° until golden brown, then cool.

Caramel sauce

4 cups heavy whipping cream
5 cups brown sugar
4 cups marshmallow cream
1 teaspoon salt
1 cup butter
4 teaspoons vanilla

Mix and cook brown sugar, marshmallow cream, heavy whipping cream, and salt. Bring to a boil. Add butter and vanilla and boil for 10 minutes. Remove from heat.

CHERRIES IN THE SNOW

A step beyond the traditional cream cheese pie, this sweet floofy dessert is enhanced with mini marshmallows for extra lift. This version comes from *Celebration A Taste of Arkansas: An Official Book of the Arkansas Sesquicentennial*.

3 ounces cream cheese (3/8 block)
1/2 cup sugar
1 teaspoon vanilla
1 cup miniature marshmallows
1/2 pint heavy cream, whipped
1-21 ounce can cherry pie filling
1 prepared 9 inch graham cracker crust

Beat first three ingredients together until fluffy. Fold in whipped cream and marshmallows. Pour into crust. Pour filling over top. Chill until ready to serve.

ZACK DIEMER'S CHERRY CREAM CHEESE PIE

My brother has the task each holiday season of creating a pie, and this is the usual suspect: the traditional cherry-pie-filling-topped favorite done large. He makes it up in a Tupperware Large White Round Storage Container (Tupperseal) that outdates both of us. The thing is thirteen inches in diameter and about three inches tall. You can substitute four eight-inch pie pans instead.

1 box graham crackers, pounded to crumbs
4-8 ounce packages cream cheese, room temperature
2-14 ounce cans sweetened condensed milk
1 tablespoon vanilla extract
1 cup lemon juice
2-21 ounce cans cherry pie filling

If you haven't done it already, beat the hell out of the graham crackers until they're big moist crumbs of graham cracker dirt. Press into the bottom of the Tupperware container. Set aside.

Beat the tar out of the cream cheese until it's sorta fluffy. Add in everything else but the cherries. Make sure the lumps are out. Slide into the fridge and let chill for four hours.

Top with the cherry pie filling and serve. If you feel really fancy, get a can of cherry pie filling and a can of blueberry pie filling and go nuts with it.

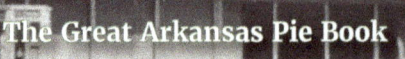

CHERRY NUT PIE

Roy Fisher's Steak House was a North Little Rock landmark for more than half a century. Opening in 1947, it served outrageously good fried chicken, salads with a proprietary dressing and pies to die for - even Elvis thought so! While the restaurant changed hands and then closed in 2005, the recipe for that incredible pie lives on. Chef Anne Wood recreated the pie from this recipe.

Crust
1-1/4 cup graham cracker crumbs
1/4 cup pecans
1/3 cup butter
1/4 cup sugar

Filling
1 -8 ounce cream cheese, softened
1-14 ounce can sweetened condensed milk
1/3 cup lemon juice
1 teaspoon vanilla extract
1/3 cup chopped pecans
1/2 cup of dark sweet cherries, pitted and cut into quarters

Combine the graham cracker crumbs, chopped pecans, melted butter and sugar and mix well. Press mixture into the bottom of a pie pan. Bake at 350° for 12 minutes. Cool completely.

In mixing bowl combine cream cheese, sweetened condensed milk, lemon juice and vanilla extract and mix well. Gently stir in pecans and cherries. Pour mixture into cooled crust. Cover and refrigerate for two to four hours before serving.

CINNAMON CREAM PIE

Franke's Cafeteria, the oldest cafeteria in Arkansas, operated from 1919 to 2020. In its century of service, it became widely known for its eggplant casserole, stuffed peppers, congealed salads, and egg custard pie. My personal Franke's favorite was this pie. I found the recipe in the 1950s *Presbyterian Cookbook*, submitted by Beverly Scull Tocum, and it comes very, very close to that rich yet fluffy dessert I loved so much.

1 and a 1/4 cup milk, divided
1/2 cup water
1/2 teaspoon nutmeg
4 rounded teaspoons cinnamon, divided
3 egg yolks
1 package unflavored gelatin
1/2 cup + 4 Tablespoons sugar, divided
3 egg whites
1 prepared 8 inch graham cracker crust
1 cup heavy cream

Scald 1 cup milk, water, nutmeg and 2 rounded teaspoons cinnamon in double boiler over simmering water. Dissolve gelatin in 1/4 cup milk. Mix gelatin into custard. Let cool.

Beat egg whites until stiff peaks form. Beat egg yolks with three tablespoons sugar until fluffy and fold into custard.

Sprinkle graham cracker crust with 1 teaspoon cinnamon. Pour custard into crust. Sprinkle 1/2 teaspoon cinnamon on top. Chill several hours.

Whip cream and remaining sugar until peaks form. Top pie. Sprinkle with remaining cinnamon. Chill until ready to serve.

COFFEE CHIFFON PIE

So, here's a secret about this pie. If you'd rather have an espresso chiffon, double the coffee powder. Want a mocha pie? Add a teaspoon of cocoa powder with the sugar when you begin. This recipe is from the Sylvan Hills High School FBLA chapter, and is featured in the *Arkansas FBLA-PBL Cookbook*.

2/3 cup sugar, divided
1 envelope or 1 teaspoon unflavored gelatin
1 Tablespoon instant coffee powder
1/4 teaspoon nutmeg
dash salt
1/2 cup heavy cream, whipped
3 slightly beaten egg yolks
1-14.5 ounce can evaporated milk
1/2 teaspoon vanilla
3 egg whites
1 baked 9-inch pastry pie shell
  or 6 baked tart shells
  or 1 chocolate graham crust

In saucepan, thoroughly combine the first 1/3 cup sugar, gelatin, coffee powder, nutmeg, and a dash of salt. Combine egg yolks and evaporated milk and stir into gelatin mixture. Cook and stir until gelatin dissolves and mixture thickens slightly. Stir in vanilla Chill til partially set, stirring frequently. Beat smooth.

Beat egg whites to soft peaks, gradually adding second 1/3 cup sugar, then fold into gelatin mixture. Pile into pie shell. Chill until firm. Top with whipped cream and chocolate curls, if desired.

Cream Pies

COCONUT CREAM LAYER PIE

The Victorian Sampler was a gorgeous tearoom housed in the old Ellis mansion near the 1886 Crescent Hotel in Eureka Springs. Though gone, its recipes live on in its eponymous cookbook, including its famed coconut cream layer pie.

2 baked 9 inch pastry pie shells
4 ounces cream cheese, softened
1 package non-dairy topping
1/2 cup milk
1 teaspoon vanilla
1 cup shredded coconut
2-3.4 ounce packages instant vanilla pudding or pie filling mix
1 teaspoon vanilla
1 cup toasted coconut
Whipped cream

Combine cream cheese, sugar, topping mix, milk and vanilla. Beat until light and fluffy. Pour into pie shells. Spread ½ cup coconut on each pie and chill several hours or overnight.

Prepare instant pie filling according to package instructions, adding one teaspoon vanilla, and pour over cream cheese layer. Chill until set. Garnish with whipped cream and toasted coconut. Makes two pies.

```
                COTTAGE CHEESE PIE

     2 packages unflavored gelatin
     3 packages Sweet & Low
     1 cup skim milk
     1 can fruit, packed in its own juice
     1 cup low calorie cottage cheese
     ½ teaspoon coconut flavoring

     Soften gelatin in ¼ cup cold water. Drain fruit and
     add enough water to juice to equal 1 cup. Heat juice
     and water to warm. Mix Sweet & Low, coconut flavor-
     ing, milk, and cottage cheese in blender. Add fruit
     juice and water to gelatin while warm. Add to blender.
     Pour into a 9" pie pan which has been sprayed with
     Pam. Decorate with fruit. Sprinkle with cinnamon
     and nutmeg.


                           Jeanne Jeffrey Huddle
```

The Great Arkansas Pie Book

FLINTROCK STRAWBERRY CREAM PIE

Ruth Moore Malone collected restaurant recipes throughout the northwest region of Arkansas and southwest Missouri in her 1964 collection *What to Eat in the Ozarks*. The book's moment in time captures so many great dishes, including this simple but absolutely excellent strawberry cream pie from Lennie's, a cafe that once served travelers and locals headed along US Highway 65 in Leslie. This strawberry pie often ended a meal of beans, greens and cornbread or a sandwich and hot coffee. I have redacted it to modern equivalents.

Cream layer
1 baked 9 inch deep dish pastry pie crust
1/2 cup sugar
2.5 Tablespoons flour
pinch salt
1 cup scalded milk or cream
2 egg yolks
1/2 teaspoon vanilla

Strawberry layer
6 cups hulled strawberries
1/3 cup sugar
1 Tablespoon lemon juice
1 Tablespoon cornstarch
Meringue of two egg whites or beaten whipped cream, optional

Stir together sugar, salt and flour. In a double boiler, heat milk or cream. Add dry ingredients Beat egg yolks and add. to milk when warm. Stir constantly until custard thickens. Add vanilla. Remove from heat and allow to cool.

Press three cups of strawberries through ricer, reserving juice. Add riced strawberries and juice to saucepan over low heat. Add sugar, lemon juice and cornstarch. Cook until thick and transparent. Fold in remaining strawberries and remove from heat. Chill.

Pour cream layer into shell, then folk strawberry glaze on top to edges of pie. Chill and let set - or - top with meringue or whipped cream and let set until ready to serve.

FRAPPUCCINO PIE

Margaret Burris made pies from her home before opening this bright little shop off Wedington Drive in Fayetteville in January 2018. Her signature pie is, frankly, all of them - which is quite fitting for a restaurant named after Margaret's three children. There are never less than three dozen pies available, and sometimes more than 50 sit in the custom cabinets and glass-front refrigerator cases around its interior. This particular pie will caffeinate you and send you along your merry way.

2 cups strong coffee
1 stick or 1-2 teaspoons instant coffee powder
1 Tablespoon butter
30 large marshmallows, cut in half
1 cup heavy cream
1/4 teaspoon coffee extract
1 baked 9 inch pastry pie crust
Whipped cream and coffee beans for garnish, if desired

In a saucepan, combine coffee, instant coffee and butter. Stir in marshmallows over medium heat until completely blended. Remove from heat and let cool.

Beat cream together with coffee extract until stiff. Fold into cooled marshmallow mixture and pour into crust. Chill four hours. Garnish if you would like.

FRESH PEACH PIE

This recipe is similar to that offered at the beloved and now gone Bryce's Cafeteria, but it still seems just a bit different. The Bryce family sold the cafeteria in Texarkana and the recipes along with it, so the original peach pie recipe is not available. Yet. Here's hoping.

1 baked 9 inch pastry pie crust
1 heaping Tablespoon cornstarch
1 cup + 1 teaspoon sugar
2 heaping Tablespoons all-purpose flour
2 cups milk
2 eggs, beaten
2 ounces (1/2 stick) butter
1 teaspoon vanilla
5 to 6 peaches, peeled and sliced
1 teaspoon lemon juice
2 cups heavy cream, whipped

In a sauce pan over medium heat, mix cornstarch, one cup of the sugar, and flour. Add milk and stir. Add eggs and stir continuously until the sauce is thickened. Add butter and vanilla. Remove from heat when butter is completely melted in. Allow to cool. Pour into crust.

Mix lemon juice and 1 teaspoon sugar. Make sure the peach slices are dry, then toss them in the lemon and sugar. Lay them out over the surface of the custard. Top with whipped cream.

FRESH PEACH PIE

This version comes from Ellen Akins, and was originally printed in *Camden's Back on Track: The Shared Recipes of Camden, Arkansas Cooks in Support of the Missouri Pacific Depot Restoration* in 1995.

1 nine inch pie shell, baked and cooled.
Whipped cream
5 to 6 large peaches, peeled and sliced thin
3/4 cup sugar
1 cup 7-Up
3 tablespoons cornstarch
1 drop red food coloring

Mix sugar, 7-Up, cornstarch and food coloring in saucepan. Cook over medium heat, stirring constantly, until custard is thick. Set custard aside to cool or cool in refrigerator. Fold in the fresh sliced peaches. Mix well with custard. Pour into pie shell. Serve with whipped cream.

GIRL SCOUT LEMON-UP PIE

My child, Hunter, created a variation on the lemon ice box pie recipe I shared in *A Bite of Arkansas* for a Girl Scout competition, using Lemon-Ups. It was really, really good! You can also use Trefoils, which is less lemon-y but just as tasty.

1 box Girl Scout Lemon-Ups
   or 1 sleeve Girl Scout Trefoils
3/4 stick butter, melted
2 Tablespoons sugar, halved
1/4 teaspoon salt
1 can sweetened condensed milk
1-8 ounce block cream cheese
zest from 1 lemon
1/4 cup lemon juice
1/2 cup heavy whipping cream
1 Tablespoon sugar

Use cookies to line outside edge of pie pan. Crush remaining cookies. Use a food processor to pulse cookies, butter, salt and a tablespoon of sugar together into fine crumbs. Place in a medium bowl. Stir in melted butter, 1 tablespoon sugar, and salt. Mix together and then press mixture into bottom and between cookies on edge of pie pan. Refrigerate until ready to fill.

Blend together sweetened condensed milk, cream cheese, lemon zest, and lemon juice until smooth. Beat whipping cream and sugar together until peaks form. Fold into cream cheese mixture. Pour into crust and refrigerate until firm (about two hours).

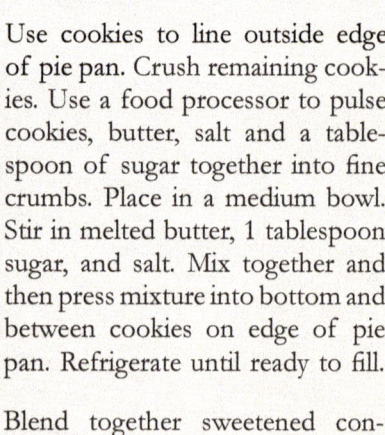

HOLIDAY SPARKLE DELIGHT PIE

R.A. Pickens and Son, founded in 1881, is a must-stop when you're in the lower Delta. The historic Commissary, still offers good country eating complete with remarkable salmon patties, fried chicken livers, smoked chicken, squash casserole, and all manners of sides and desserts. There are always homemade pies in the refrigerated case by the kitchen. Miss Kim's pretty pie here is perfect for adapting to any holiday, with just a switch of the food coloring you use.

1 large can lemonade frozen concentrate, partially thawed
2 cans Eagle Brand sweetened condensed milk
3 small containers Cool Whip
Food coloring of choice
3 prepared graham cracker crusts

Blend together concentrate and milk. Add 3-6 drops of your food coloring of choice. Fold in Cool Whip. Lay into graham cracker crusts. Place in the freezer until an hour before use. Garnish if desired.

Tip: Use a knife run under hot water to slice.

The Great Arkansas Pie Book

LEMON ICE CREAM PIE

Susan Speake of Little Rock submitted this recipe for *Calico Cupboards*, the 1980 cookbook by the Benton Junior Axillary

1 pint vanilla ice cream
1 - 6 ounce can frozen lemonade
1 - 8 ounce container Cool Whip
Sliced lemon for garnish
Yellow food coloring
Graham cracker crust

Let vanilla ice cream soften. Cream together ice cream and frozen lemonade. Blend in Cool Whip. Add food coloring and blend until desired color is reached. Pour into graham cracker crust and freeze at least one hour Garnish with sliced lemon and more Cool Whip.

LEMON IMPROV PIE

When I was promoting *Arkansas Pie: A Delicious Slice of The Natural State*, back in 2012, I had one morning where I found out at the very last minute I needed a pie to bring to a TV station Lacking ingredients, I threw this together - and much to my surprise, it worked!

6 ounces cookies of choice
   (lemon sandwich, ginger snaps,
   oatmeal or sugar wafers)
1 stick butter, melted

1-8 ounce block cream cheese
1-14 ounce can sweetened
   condensed milk
1/3 cup lemon juice

Beat cookies into crumbs, then fold in melted butter. Press into 9 inch pie plate. Blend together milk, cream cheese and lemon juice and pour into crust. Freeze for one hour.

LEMON RICE PIE

Edith Underwood shared this surprisingly filling yet light pie in *The Art of Cooking in Heber Spring*s by the Cleburne County Senior Citizens.

2 egg yolks
1 and a 1/2 cup boiled rice
1/2 cup lemon juice

1 can Eagle Brand condensed milk
1 cup Cool Whip
1 prepared graham cracker crust

Mix everything except the pie crust and pour it into the pie crust. Top with meringue or whipped topping, if desired.

LUSCIOUS LEMON PIE

Elizabeth McMullen graciously shared three of her pie recipes for this book. The woman behind the venerable E's Bistro offers, amongst the others, this divine lemony dream.

1 cup sugar
1/4 cup butter
1/2 teaspoon salt
rind of one lemon
3 Tablespoons cornstarch
1/3 cup fresh lemon juice
3 egg yolks
1 cup sour cream
1 baked 9 inch pie crust
1/3 cup heavy cream
3 Tablespoons confectioners' sugar
1 teaspoon almond flavoring

Combine first seven ingredients. Cook in saucepan over medium heat until thickened, stirring constantly. Cool in refrigerator one hour.

Fold sour cream into lemon mixture. Turn out into pie crust.

Beat together cream, confectioners' sugar and flavoring until soft peas form. Spoon or pipe over top of pie. Refrigerate pie several hours before serving.

Cream Pies

MANDARIN ORANGE PIE

This fluffy pie, similar to a Millionaire Pie, was contributed to the *Alexander Human Development Center Volunteer Council Cookbook* by Sarah Dillard of Little Rock.

1 medium can crushed pineapple, drained
1 medium can mandarin oranges, drained
1/4 cup lemon juice
1 can Eagle Brand condensed milk
1 - 8 ounce carton Cool Whip
1 prepared graham cracker crust

Mix ingredients well and pour into crust. Chill in refrigerator at least two hours before serving.

MELLOW MAI TAI PIE

Dee Dee Frazider submitted this tropical delight for *Camden's Back on Track: The Shared Recipes of Camden, Arkansas Cooks in Support of the Missouri Pacific Depot Restoration*, printed in 1995.

1 pint pineapple or lemon sherbet
1/4 cup lime juice
1 Tablespoon lemon juice
1 teaspoon grated orange peel
1-20 ounce can crushed pineapple, drained
1 pint vanilla ice cream, softened

2 Tablespoons orange juice
1 Tablespoon grated lime peel
1 Teaspoon grated lemon peel

Macaroon crust

2 cups macaroon cookie crumbles
1/4 cup butter, melted

Combine macaroon cookie crumb and butter. Press into 10 inch pie plate. Refrigerate until ready to use.

Combine softened sherbet and ice cream with all juices and grated peel. Fold in pineapple. Pour into macaroon crust. Freeze until firm or overnight. Garnish with pineapple slices and lime slices, if desired.

MILLIONAIRE PIE

Furr's Cafeteria started in San Antonio, Texas in 1946. Its Fort Smith location was a popular local draw up until the closure of the entire franchise in 2021. This is the recipe for Furr's famous Millionaire pie.

2 cups powdered sugar
2 egg yolks
1/2 teaspoon vanilla extract
1/2 cup pecans, chopped
1/2 cup butter, softened

1/4 teaspoon salt
1 cup crushed pineapple, drained
2 cups whipping cream
2 baked deep dish pie crusts

In a large bowl, cream together butter, powdered sugar, egg yolks, salt and vanilla extract. Beat until it resembles frosting. Spread mixture into pie shells. Chill while you prepare the next layer.

In a large bowl, whip whipping cream until stiff peaks form. Blend in crushed pineapple and pecans. Spread on top of first layer. Chill for 3 hours or more.

Cream Pies

KOPPER KETTLE SMOKEHOUSE MILLIONAIRE PIE

Next door to the famous Kopper Kettle Candies on US Highway 64 between Alma and Van Buren, there's this marvelous smokehouse and lunchroom, where decadent sandwiches are served on soft bread and there are always so many pies to choose from - including this classic Millionaire pie.

2-8 ounce blocks cream cheese
1-1/2 cups confectioners' sugar
1-1/2 cups Cool Whip
1/4 cup crushed pineapple
1/4 cup pecan pieces
1/2 cup coconut
1 prepared 9 inch graham cracker crust

Mix cream cheese and powdered sugar until well blended. Fold in the rest of the ingredients to the cream cheese and spoon into crust. Chill.

MELINDA'S NO-BAKE CHEESE CHIFFON PIE

My friend Melinda LaFevers, an author, re-enactor and general good egg., has collected a lot of recipes over the years, including a handy cheese chiffon pie that can be augmented in so many ways.

1-8 ounce package cream cheese, softened
1/2 pint heavy whipping cream
Sugar to taste, 1/2 to 1 cup (powdered or granulated is fine)
1/2 teaspoon vanilla flavoring
Graham cracker crust or your favorite pie crust
Optional: canned pie filling, fresh or canned fruit (blueberries, cherries, strawberries)

Prepare pie crust. Cream together cream cheese, sugar and vanilla. Whip cream and fold into cheese mixture. Refrigerate until set. If desired, top with pie filling or fresh or canned fruit before serving.

For a heavier pie and more of a cheese taste, use two packages of cream cheese. For a lighter fluffier pie, use a full pint of whipping cream. For a caramel cheese chiffon, boil an unopened can of sweetened condensed milk for three hours (make sure it stays covered with water or it could explode) let cool, and use in place of sugar.

PEANUT BUTTER PIE

This version is served at the Oark General Store in Oark.

1 cup peanut butter
1/2 cup confectioners' sugar
1/4 cup milk
8 ounce block cream cheese
8 ounces Cool Whip
1/2 of a 14.3 ounce package Oreos
2 Tablespoons melted butter

Process Oreos into powder in food processor. Combine with butter and press into 9 inch pie pan. Mix all remaining ingredients except Cool Whip until smooth, then fold in Cool Whip. Lay peanut butter mixture into center of crust and work it out to the edges. Chill.

Cream Pies

PEACH VANILLA CREAM PIE

6 whole graham cracker planks, pounded to crumbs
1 Tablespoon butter
1-8 ounce package cream cheese at room temperature
1/2 can sweetened condensed milk
2 teaspoons vanilla
1 Tablespoon lemon juice
4 fresh ripe peaches, sliced

Melt butter. Blend together graham cracker crumbs with butter, then press into pie pan. Set aside.

Blend together cream cheese, sweetened condensed milk, vanilla and lemon juice. Pour into pie crust. Place peach slices on top. Cover and refrigerate until ready to serve.

Variation: Melt together 1 Tablespoon butter, 1 Tablespoon brown sugar and 1 teaspoon vanilla. Fold in peach slices. Array peach mixture atop cream cheese filling. Cover and refrigerate until ready to serve.

PEANUT BUTTER CREAM PIE

Susan Foster's version of this cream cheese-based peanut butter pie is a good one to make and freeze in advance for later.

3 ounces cream cheese
1 cup confectioners' sugar
1/3 cup peanut butter
1/4 cup milk
4-1/2 ounces whipped topping
1 prepared 8 inch graham cracker pie crust

Whip cream cheese until fluffy. Beat in sugar and peanut butter. Slowly add milk, blending thoroughly into the mixture. Gently fold (do not stir) topping into mixture. Pour into pie crust. Sprinkle with chopped peanuts, if desired. Chill for at least one hour.

Cream Pies

PEANUT BUTTER ICE CREAM PIE

Whether it's at the Pine Bluff Country Club, UAPTC's Culinary Arts and Hospitality Management Institute, or one of the dozens upon dozens of events he caters throughout Arkansas, Chef Jamie McAfee brings South Arkansas to the table. The McGehee native's time in gardens, kitchens and out hunting and fishing as a child and young man shines through dishes such as Frog Legs Glacé, fried green tomatoes topped with grilled shrimp and remoulade, and both peanut butter and peppermint ice cream pies that date back to 1914.

Crust
1-1/2 cups graham cracker crumbs
1 Tablespoon sugar
1/3 cup butter, softened

Filling
1 quart vanilla ice cream
1/2 cup crunchy peanut butter
1/4 cup heavy cream, whipped

Mix crumbs, sugar and butter and press into a 9 inch pie plate. Chill.

Beat ice cream and peanut butter until soft. Fold in whipped cream. Turn into crust; freeze until firm.

LORETTA'S PEANUT BUTTER PIE

The Shake Shack in Marion has a reputation for extraordinary pies, including a hot fudge pie that's received a lot of attention, gorgeous lattice-top pies, crazy pies such as the Tang pie, and my favorite, the caramel apple fried pie. This neat entry is a peanut butter pie enhanced with Nutter Butter cookies. It's remarkably easy to make.

1 - 16 ounce package Nutter Butter peanut butter sandwich cookies
1 - 3 ounce package Nutter Butter Bites miniature sandwich cookies
5 Tablespoons melted butter
8 ounces sour cream
1 cup peanut butter
1 can Eagle Brand sweetened condensed milk
1-8 ounce carton Cool Whip

Crush full size Nutter Butter cookies in food processor. Add butter. Press into two pie pans. Freeze.

Mix remaining ingredients together and pour into pie crust. Line outside edge with miniature Nutter Butter cookies. Refrigerate until ready to serve.

Cream Pies

PEPPERMINT ICE BOX PIE

In *Our Favorite Recipes* by the Antioch Baptist Church of Springfield, Jan Sumner shares this creamy but thick holiday pie that showcases the glorious candy cane.

Filling

1-1/2 eight ounce blocks cream cheese
1-7 ounce container marshmallow creme
1 Tablespoon peppermint extract
1-1/2 cups heavy cream
3/4 cup confectioners' sugar
5 drops red food coloring
2 candy canes, crushed
1 prepared 8 inch chocolate graham cracker crust

Topping

1 cup heavy cream
1/4 cup confectioners' sugar
2 candy canes, crushed

Beat cream cheese until smooth. Add marshmallow creme and peppermint extract and beat until blended. Separately, beat together the heavy cream, sugar and food coloring until stiff; fold into the marshmallow mixture along with the candy canes. Spoon into crust and chill overnight.

To top, whip cream and confectioners' sugar until stiff. Fold in candy cane bits .Spoon or pipe onto pie. Serve immediately or freeze.

PEPPERMINT ICE CREAM PIE

One of the two 1914 dated desserts on Chef Jamie McAfee's menu at the Pine Bluff Country Club - this is a particularly welcome experience, particularly during one of our typically steamy Arkansas summers.

Crust
1-4 ounce bar German's sweet baking chocolate
4 Tablespoons butter
3 cups Rice Krispies

Filling
1/2 gallon vanilla ice cream, softened
3/4 cup crushed peppermint candies

Into saucepan over medium heat, break chocolate into pieces; add butter, stir until melted. Remove from heat and add Rice Krispies. Mix well. Press into bottom and sides of 10 inch pie plate. Refrigerate.

Break candies into very small pieces; stir into ice cream. Put filling in crust and freeze until firm, 3-4 hours.

STRAWBERRY CREAM PIE

Another version of the classic cream cheese pie. Here, the cream cheese retains a lovely light lemon flavor with great balance. Also, as you can see here, you can substitute whipped cream from a can but you might not like the visuals. It eats, though.

1 baked 9 inch graham cracker crust
3 ounces cream cheese, room temperature
1 quart strawberries, rinsed and hulled
1 cup sugar
5 Tablespoons cornstarch
1 Tablespoon lemon juice
Whipped cream or topping

Spread bottom of baked crust with cream cheese. Fill with whole berries, stem side down, in a single layer. Take remaining berries and cook down with lemon juice, cornstarch and sugar until translucent sauce thickens. Allow to cool to room temperature, then pour over berries. Refrigerate. Serve with whipped cream or whipped topping.

RASPBERRY CREAM CHEESE PIE

Third generation Little Rock restaurateur Capi Peck is the closest thing Arkansas has to restaurant royalty. Her flagship restaurant, Trio's, has served the city since 1986. Every diner receives a chance to view the heavily-laden dessert tray - and more often than not, it's this sweet-and-tart pie that gets chosen.

Crust
1-1/4 cups vanilla wafer crumbs
2 Tablespoons sugar
6 Tablespoons melted butter
1/2 cup chopped pecans

Filling
1 block cream cheese, softened
1/2 cup confectioners' sugar
1 teaspoon vanilla
2 Tablespoons Triple Sec
1 cup heavy cream

Topping
2-1/2 cups frozen raspberries
1 cup sugar
4 Tablespoons water, divided
2 heaping Tablespoons cornstarch

For crust: Heat oven to 350°. Place cookie crumbs, sugar, butter and pecans in mixing bowl and work with fingers until well-combined. Press into bottoms and sides of 9 inch pie pan. Bake 8 minutes. Let cool.

For filling: Beat cream cheese and sugar together until light and fluffy. Add vanilla and Triple Sec and incorporate. In separate bowl, beat cream until soft peaks begin to form. Fold into cream cheese mixture. Spoon into crust.

For topping: Place raspberries, sugar and 2 tablespoons water in a saucepan over medium high heat. Let mixture come to a full boil, stirring constantly. Raspberries will fall apart. Dissolve cornstarch in remaining water, then stir into raspberry sauce. Continue to cook and stir until raspberry sauce thickens. Remove from heat and cool completely. Spread over pie, cover, and chill several hours before serving.

Cream Pies

SUGAR MILK CREAM PIE

Pea Farm Bistro in Cabot is well known for its sandwiches and lunches and for an extraordinary peanut butter pie. This sugar cream pie from Justin and Andrea Wilson is a sheer delight.

Crust

2-1/2 cups all purpose flour
2 Tablespoons sugar
1 teaspoon salt
1/2 cup cold unsalted butter
1/2 cup cold shortening
1/2 cup cold water

Mix dry ingredients. Cut in butter and shortening. Add in cold water, gently. Mix by hand until dough forms. Roll and chill 2 hours.

Custard

1 cup sugar
1/2 cup cornstarch
Pinch salt
2-1/2 cups heavy cream
3 Tablespoons unsalted butter
2 teaspoons vanilla

Whisk together sugar, salt, and cornstarch. In pot over medium heat, pour cream and whisk in dry ingredients. Whisk until mixture reaches pudding consistency (about 30 minutes). Remove from heat. Whisk in butter and vanilla. Chill and spoon into pie crust. You may broil or torch top for a creme Brule upper crust.

CHESS and CUSTARD PIES

BLUEBERRY CHESS PIE

Kelli Marks is well known for her extraordinary baking in our neck of the woods. Her wedding cakes are pure treasures, but her pies... well, she makes some of the greatest. This one, she has thoughts on.

"This pie recipe is a favorite; I find myself dreaming about it sometimes. It's a medley of flavors and textures that join into a perfect symphony of a dessert. The flavors and presentation are complex enough to follow up the most impressive meal, but the steps are simple enough that you can whip one up for a casual weekday dessert."

1 unbaked 9 inch pie crust
1 cup blueberries (fresh is best, but frozen are fine)
1/2 cup unsalted butter, melted
1-1/4 cup granulated sugar
2 Tablespoons almond flour
2 Tablespoons flour
1/4 teaspoon salt
4 eggs
1/2 cup buttermilk
2 Tablespoons lemon juice
1 teaspoon vanilla
Zest of 1 lemon
Additional sugar for top of pie

Preheat oven to 350°. Place the blueberries into the bottom of the unbaked pie shell.

Combine melted butter and sugar, followed by remaining ingredients. Whisk after each ingredient is included. Pour filling into pie crust, over the top of the blueberries.

Bake for 45 minutes. If the edges of the pie begin to get too dark, carefully cover crust with foil or pie shield.

Pie is ready when center has a slight jiggle. Allow to cool on counter and then transfer to the refrigerator.

When ready to serve, top the pie with a layer of granulated sugar and brulee with a torch or carefully on the broil setting in the oven. Do not leave in the oven too long; this pie is best served chilled.

If you are not serving the entire pie, brulee each slice individually. The pie is best with a fresh crunchy layer of bruleed sugar. Keep leftover pie in the refrigerator.

Tip: If you have a nut allergy, replace the 2 tablespoons. almond flour with 1 additional tablespoon. of flour..

Chess and Custard Pies

BROWN SUGAR BUTTERMILK PIE

There's nothing quite like a buttermilk pie - particularly one made with fresh buttermilk You can't get a fresher buttermilk pie than the one offered at Dogwood Hills Guest Farm - since the buttermilk is cultured in the kitchen above the stall where the cows are milked. Pair with a gluten-free crust or all-butter flour crust for a humble yet noble slice.

1 unbaked 9 inch all butter pie crust
3 large eggs + 2 egg yolks
3 Tablespoons gluten-free flour
1 cup dark brown sugar, packed
1-1/2 cups buttermilk
1/2 to 3/4 teaspoon fresh grated nutmeg
1/4 to 1/2 teaspoon cinnamon
6 Tablespoons melted butter

Heat oven to 350°. Bake crust lined with parchment and baking beans for 10 minutes.

While the crust bakes, whisk together all remaining ingredients except butter. Slowly pour in butter. Immediately pour batter into pie shell and bake 35 minutes. The pie should be lightly golden and slightly wobbly in the center. Cool completely, then chill overnight or eight hours.

Chess and Custard Pies

BROWN SUGAR PIE

Jody Melton with the Lonoke FBLA submitted this recipe for the *Arkansas FBLA-PBL Cookbook*. It's similar to a pecan pie, but without the nuts.

- 2 cups brown sugar
- 2 eggs
- 4 Tablespoons milk
- 3 Tablespoons flour
- 1/2 cup melted butter
- 1 teaspoon vanilla
- 1 unbaked 9 inch pastry pie crust

Mix sugar and flour. Add eggs and milk. Stir. Pour in butter and blend well. Add vanilla Pour into crust and bake 45-50 minutes at 350°.

BROWN SUGAR PIE

Tandra Watkins served as pastry chef at the revered Capital Hotel's top tier restaurant, Ashley's at the Capital, and even earned a James Beard Award nomination in the position. This particular pie was one of the star attractions of the dessert menu.

As she shared in *Arkansas Pie: A Delicious Slice of The Natural State*, "I received this pie recipe from Chef Bill Smith of Crook's Corner in Chappell Hill, NC. It is adapted from one of Nancy McDermott's recipes (the pie maven of the south). The brown sugar custard puts the 'Goo' in Good. Once you try it, you'll never be able to live without it!"

Pie Dough

1-1/4 cup all purpose flour
1/2 cup cake flour
1-1/2 teaspoons kosher salt
2 Tablespoons powdered sugar
4 ounces Crisco shortening, cold

4 ounces unsalted butter, cold and cut into cubes
1 large egg
1 Tablespoon white vinegar
4 ounces ice water

In a food processor, process all the dry ingredients to whisk them together. Then add the Crisco and butter, pulse the mixture together until the butter is in little pea sized pieces. Add the egg, vinegar and some of the water and start the machine, and slowly add the rest of the water. Stop the machine as soon as the dough starts to come together into a ball. Turn the dough out onto a floured work surface and shape it into a disk. Wrap the dough with plastic wrap and chill for at least 2 hours.

To prepare the pie shell, flour a work surface and roll the chilled dough out 1/4" thick. Transfer the dough to a 9" pie pan and press the dough into the bottom and corners of the pie pan. Trim the excess dough th at hangs over the edge of the pan, about 1/2" past the lip of the pan. Tuck the overhang of dough just inside the edge of the pan and crimp the dough to your liking. Place the prepared pie shell in the freezer to set while you prepare the filling.

Place the prepared pie shell in the freezer to set while you prepare the filling. Preheat the oven to 350°F (or 325°F for convection).

Chess and Custard Pies

Brown Sugar Custard

1 pound light brown sugar
4 large eggs
1/4 cup whole milk

1/2 Tablespoon pure vanilla extract
1/4 teaspoon kosher salt
4 ounces unsalted butter, melted

In a food processor or a stand mixer fitted with a whisk attachment, blend together the light brown sugar, eggs, milk, vanilla, and salt until completely blended and smooth. With the machine running, slowly stream in the melted butter until it is all mixed in well.

Pour the custard into the prepared pie shell and bake at 350° (325° for convection) for 30- 40 minutes, or until the pie is puffed and golden brown, if shaken will jiggle a little bit but will not be liquid at all. Allow the pie to cool completely before cutting and serving with the bourbon whipped cream.

Buttermilk Pie

1½ C white sugar
2 heaping T AP flour
⅛–¼ t. nutmeg (depends on freshness)
pinch salt
— whisk together in med. bowl

Add:
3 large eggs
1 cup Bulgarian buttermilk
2 t Watkins vanilla
½ c melted unsalted butter

Pour into unbaked 9" deep dish pie crust. Use crust protector. Bake @ 350° for 35–40 min. It'll look unfinished but will set up as it cools.

Pie Crust:
2 C WR brand AP flour
1 t salt
1 C butter crisco
⅓ – ½ cup ice H₂O

This recipe comes from Jennifer Richardson Jones of the exemplary Big Springs Trading Company in St. Joe.

Chess and Custard Pies

CANNOLI PIE

Dogwood Hills Guest Farm isn't just a place where you can go, stay and milk a cow. It's become a remarkable center of celebration for local food and the budding agritourism movement here in Arkansas. Mother-daughter team Ruth and Grace Pepler run not only the unusual one-family-at-a-time accommodations but also a budding microdairy and an entirely gluten-free kitchen that produces pastries, personalized breakfasts and prime farm-to-table dinners.

I've rather enjoyed watching the Peplers - Ruth, Grace, and Thomas - make these great strides towards creating this wonderful place. Their hospitality has always been a great respite from the busy media-filled world of our cities and highways, and I'm heartened to know whenever I climb up to that loft kitchen, there's always a cup of coffee, a bite to eat and a great conversation waiting for me.

This cannoli pie can be made in your home - but when it's made at Dogwood Hills, it's made using ricotta cultured from the very milk of the farm's cows, fed from fodder grown within eyesight of the kitchen window, one of the shortest food-mile treats you'll find anywhere.

Crust
1 unbaked 9 inch deep dish pastry pie crust (gluten-free on page 24)
2 teaspoons butter
2 teaspoons Marsala wine
pinch cinnamon

Topping
Toasted chopped pistachios
Confectioners' sugar

Filling
3 extra large eggs
15 ounces whole milk ricotta
1 teaspoon vanilla
12 ounces confectioners' sugar
& 8 ounces heavy cream
OR 1-14 ounce can sweetened condensed milk
3/4 cup mini chocolate chips
2 teaspoon flour

Chess and Custard Pies

Preheat oven to 350°. Place crust in pie pan. Mix together butter and wine and brush crust, then sprinkle crust with cinnamon. Set aside. Toss mini chips together with two teaspoons flour. Also set aside.

In a large bowl, whisk eggs, ricotta and vanilla well. Stir in condensed milk or cream/sugar mixture. Fold in the chips. Pour into the pie shell Sprinkle the pistachios around the edge next to the crust. Bake 55-60 minutes. Cool then chill. Dust with powdered sugar just before serving.

CATHIE'S BUTTERMILK PIE

Cathie Brown walked in the back door at the Oark General Store one day, and she never left. She started making pies and biscuits for the oldest general store in the state and the little cafe the Eisele's started there, and soon was being hailed for her baking prowess. She passed in 2022, but the Oark General Store has graciously shared several recipes, including this one for her buttermilk pie. It makes two.

6 eggs
3-3/4 cups sugar
1 teaspoon cinnamon
1 cup buttermilk

1 cup butter, softened
1 teaspoon vanilla
1/2 all-purpose flour
2 unbaked pastry pie crusts

Heat oven to 350°. Cream eggs and sugar together. Add each ingredient and mix in-between, in order. Pour into pie crusts and bake 45 minutes to one hour. Center will be giggly. Cool completely.

Chess and Custard Pies

CHESS PIE

The name of this dessert is a bastardization of its real name, "just pie." When you're broke and have nothing more for filling... or if you're aching for the simplicity of earlier times, chess pie is for you. This recipe comes from the University of Arkansas Library, attributed to Ruth Chastang in 1978.

1 unbaked 8-inch pie shell
3 large eggs
1 and a half cups sugar
1 Tablespoon cornmeal
1 Tablespoon vinegar
1/2 cup butter, melted
1 Tablespoon vanilla

Beat eggs with fork until light; add sugar, cornmeal and vinegar. Stir to mix well but do not beat. Add cooled butter and vanilla; stir to mix well. Pour into pie shell. Bake at 350° for 60 to 65 minutes.

TESSIE'S CHESS PIE

Another recipe comes from *Boilin' n' Bakin' in Booger Hollow*, the 1971 cookbook from the beloved tourist attraction, presented in the vernacular of the book.

1 cuppa sugar
3 beat aigs
1/4 pound butter
1 Tablespoon cornmeal
1 1/2 teaspoon vinegar
1/2 teaspoon vanilly

Melt the butter n' add all the rest of the ingredimints. Mix hit all up'n pour unto an uncooked pastry. Cook until kinda firm.

COCONUT PIE

Cooking Favorites of Tomberlin is a community cookbook from the England community, east of Little Rock. It contains this recipe from Mrs. Eugene Neal Sr. This is a not-too-rich but comforting pie that had no leftovers on my trial runs. Don't chill the filling before adding the meringue. Double the egg whites for a fluffier, taller top.

1/2 cup flour
1/2 cup water
3 egg yolks, well beaten
1-1/2 cups + 1 teaspoon sugar
2-1/2 cups milk
2/3 stick butter

2 cups flaked coconut (plus extra for topping)
1 Tablespoon vanilla
3 egg whites (more to make taller)
1/8 teaspoon cream of tartar
1 large baked pastry pie shell

Mix flour and water to make paste. Add egg yolks; beat well. Add 1 1/2 cups sugar and milk. Cook over low heat, stirring constantly, until thickened. Add coconut, butter and vanilla. Pour into pie shell

Beat egg whites until foamy, then add remaining sugar and cream of tartar. Beat until stiff peaks form. Top pie with meringue. Sprinkle a little coconut over meringue. Bake at 350° until brown.

Variation: Omit 1/2 cup milk and coconut. Substitute with 1/2 cup cocoa dissolved in 1/2 cup hot water.

Chess and Custard Pies

> 3 eggs Whole
> 1 1/4 cups sugar fine
> 1 can fine coconut
> 1 stick Oleo milted
> 1/4 cup buttermilk
> 1 tea Vanilla
>
> Mix and pour into unbaked pie crust for 35 Min 5.0

Above: a recipe for a coconut custard pie found tucked in a 1953 El Dorado cookbook.

CORNMEAL PIE

Erma Moody contributed this to the *Alpena Cooks* cookbook, utilizing cornmeal as its base.

1 cup brown sugar
2 eggs, slightly beaten
1 heaping Tablespoon cornmeal
2 Tablespoons flour
1 cup sugar
1/2 cup milk
1 teaspoon vanilla
1/2 stick butter
1 unbaked 9 inch pastry pie crust

Mix well and place in pie shell and bake 375° about 40 minutes. Comes out like a Karo nut pie.

CUSHAW PIE

Everyone knows about pumpkin pie, and some know about squash pie, but there aren't a lot of people outside of Arkansas who delve into good old cushaw pie. These large crook-necked green and white gourds are often used today as an ornamental during the fall. But they also make a very good pie filling. Just roast and mash before beginning this recipe.

This pie is served at the Williams Tavern Restaurant on the grounds of Historic Washington State Park, north of Hope. The tavern building itself is one of the oldest extant restaurant buildings in the state.

2 cups cushaw squash, roasted and pureed
2/3 cup brown sugar
1 teaspoon ground cinnamon
1/2 teaspoon ground ginger
1/2 teaspoon salt
3 large eggs
1 teaspoon vanilla
1-12 ounce can evaporated milk
1 unbaked 9 inch pastry pie crust

Combine cushaw squash puree, brown sugar, cinnamon, ginger, and salt in a medium-size mixing bowl. Add eggs and vanilla, then beat lightly with a whisk. Stir in evaporated milk. Mix well. Pour into a pastry-lined pie plate. Bake on the lowest oven rack at 375° for 50-60 minutes, until a toothpick inserted in the center comes out clean. Chill before serving.

Chess and Custard Pies

DANG GOOD PIE

Somewhere around 2011, I encountered my first slice of Dang Good Pie. It was at 302 on the Square, Alexander Virden's restaurant on the first floor of the old Grand View hotel on the Berryville town square. He told us, as Grav and I shared a slice, that the recipe dated back to the Civil War. Well, I didn't get that recipe from him, but I did find this version in *Recipes and Remembrances*, submitted by Glenda Gaines.

3/4 stick butter
3 eggs, beaten
3 Tablespoons flour
1-1/2 cup sugar
1 cup crushed pineapple
1 cup coconut flakes
1 unbaked 9 inch pastry pie crust

Mix dry ingredients. Melt butter and mix with remaining ingredients. Pour into shell. Bake at 350° for one hour or until brown on top.

DREAMSICLE PIE

The Root Cafe has become one of Little Rock's most noted destination dining spots. Its commitment to locally sourced produce and meats, environmentally friendly practices and recycling are laudable enough. The extraordinary dishes served in the old Sweeden Creme elevate it to a place you absolutely have to try. The desserts change with the season, but this Dreamsicle pie from Chef Jonathan Arrington is a pie for all seasons.

Crust

- 1-1/2 cups crushed graham crackers
- 1/4 cup light brown sugar
- 1 teaspoon kosher salt
- 1 Tablespoon ground coriander
- 1/2 cup melted butter

Heat conventional oven to 350°. If using a convection oven set to 300° with the vent closed and the fan on low.

Combine dry ingredients in a mixing bowl. Stir in melted butter. The mixture should feel like wet sand.

Spray your 9 inch pie plate with non-stick spray. Dump most of the graham cracker mix in there and start to pat it down in the bottom of the pie plate. Be careful to not press down too firmly so that the crust doesn't get too hard. Run some of the crust up the side of the pie plate and gently press to form the side crust. Run the back of a spoon around the bottom of the pie plate where the bottom and side crust meet to form a rounded edge. You will have some crust left over; save for garnish. Bake in the preheated oven for about 10 minutes. Allow to cool at room temperature.

Filling

- 8 egg yolks
- 1-14 ounce can sweetened condensed milk
- 1 cup heavy cream
- 4 ounces white chocolate
- 1 teaspoon kosher salt
- 2 Tablespoons orange zest (zest of 4 oranges)
- 1/2 cup orange juice (juice of 4 oranges)

Separate your yolks and have them hanging out in a mixing bowl.

Heat the heavy cream and white chocolate on low heat until chocolate is melted. Combine with condensed milk, salt, zest, and juice and blend until smooth, about 30 seconds. Slowly stir pureed mixture into egg yolks. Gently pour custard into pie shell. Place pie plate on a half sheet tray and bake in preheated oven for 45-50 minutes. Gently shake the sheet tray to check for doneness. The center of the pie should have a slight jiggle and be nicely browned on top.

Chill at least four hours or preferably overnight. Serve with whipped cream and some of the leftover crust mixture.

Chess and Custard Pies

DUTCH VANILLA CREAM PIE

A different take on a traditional cream pie, this one comes from Dorothy Swarts of the Daniel Economic Homemakers Council chapter in the 1993 publication *The Good Cooks Book - Garland County Extension Homemakers Council.*

1 cup sugar
1/2 cup white corn syrup
1 cup + 1/2 tablespoon flour
1 cup water
1 egg
1/2 tablespoon vanilla
1 unbaked 9 inch pastry pie crust
1/4 cup shortening
1/2 teaspoon baking soda
1/2 teaspoon cream of tartar

Heat half a cup sugar, corn syrup, half a tablespoon flour, water, egg, and vanilla to boiling. Pour into unbaked pie crust. Prepare a crumb topping by combining 1 cup flour, half a cup sugar, shortening, baking soda and cream of tartar. Put crumb topping on pie, and bake at 350° for 40-45 minutes.

ANDERSON'S EGG CUSTARD PIE

From its opening in 1953, Anderson's Restaurant in Beebe was known for pies that Alberta Plummer and Carrie Pruitt created. The coconut pie appears on page 178 - this here is the famed egg custard from the restaurant.

1/2 cup unsalted butter, softened
1 cup granulated sugar
Pinch of salt
5 eggs
2 cups milk
1 teaspoon vanilla
1 unbaked 9 inch pastry pie shell
Ground nutmeg

Heat oven to 350°. In a large bowl, beat together the butter, sugar, and salt. Beat in eggs. Add milk and vanilla until mixture is smooth. Pour into pie shell and sprinkle nutmeg over top. Bake for 40 to 45 minutes or until filling is firm.

FRANKE'S EGG CUSTARD PIE

Elizabeth Elizandro shares this handwritten recipe from her mother, Carol Parten of Russellville, for the famed egg custard pie from Franke's Cafeteria.

> **Recipe for:** Franke's Egg Custard Pie
> **Ingredients:**
> 1 C. sugar   2 T. oleo   6 whole eggs
> 1/8 t. salt   1/8 t. nutmeg or more   1/2 t. vanilla
>
> Mix sugar, oleo, salt & nutmeg. Add whole eggs. Beat well. Add milk & vanilla. Beat. Bake 7 minutes at 425°. Lower heat to 325° & bake for 20-25 minutes or until knife comes out clean.

The Great Arkansas Pie Book

FRANKE'S EGG CUSTARD PIE

This book would not be complete without a recipe for that holy grail of pies, the egg custard pie from Franke's. The oldest cafeteria in Arkansas closed for good during the pandemic, just over a hundred years after first opening in downtown Little Rock.

Many, many, many cookbooks purport to have the exact recipe. In fairness to all, I've tried out half a dozen, and this one seems closest of all - one sent to me by Julie Myrick.

Crust
2 cups flour
3/4 cup Crisco
1 Tablespoon Karo light corn syrup
1 Tablespoon egg white
6 Tablespoons water

Filling
3/4 cup sugar
2 Tablespoons butter
1/2 teaspoon freshly grated nutmeg
1/4 teaspoon salt
6 eggs
2 cups cold milk

Cut flour and Crisco together until pebbles form. Add in corn syrup and egg white. Work in water, one tablespoon at a time, until dough comes together. Refrigerate until ready to roll out and use. Bake crust in 10 inch pie shell for 10 minutes at 400° and let cool before filling.

Heat oven to 475°. Mix nutmeg and salt into butter. Cream eggs into butter, adding one at a time. Stir in milk. Pour into pie shell and bake 7 minutes, then reduce heat to 325° and bake an additional 20 minutes. Don't overcook. Center will shimmy when shaken.

EGG CUSTARD PIE

This version belonged to Anne Hodges Peterson and was submitted by her daughter, Carol Hix.

1/3 stick butter
1 cup sugar
1/4 teaspoon salt
1/2 teaspoon or more nutmeg

2-1/4 cups whole milk
1 teaspoon vanilla
5 eggs
1 unbaked 9 inch pastry pie crust

Mix butter, sugar, salt, nutmeg and milk and heat until very warm and add to mixing bowl. Turn mixer on high and add eggs one at a time beating about 2 minutes until frothy on top. Add vanilla. Pour into pie shell and bake at 400°for 15-20 minutes until knife inserted is clean. DO NOT OVERBAKE. Pie should jiggle in the middle when it is done..

EGG CUSTARD PIE

Youth Homes, Incorporated has published a number of cookbooks over the years. Back in the 1980s, the private agency that works to rehabilitate severely disturbed teenagers in central Arkansas, operated a tearoom and gift shop known as the Yellow Daisy. This recipe comes from *Lunch at the Yellow Daisy II*, published in 1982.

1-1/2 cup sugar
2 Tablespoons butter
dash salt
1 teaspoon nutmeg
1-2/3 cup whole milk
4 eggs
1 unbaked 9 inch pastry pie crust

Mix all ingredients well and pour into pie shell. Bake 7 minutes at 425° degrees, then 50 minutes at 325° degrees.

EGG CUSTARD PIE

And yet another Franke's custard pie recipe, this one from Mrs. Homer Keel, Sr. from the El Dorado *Presbyterian Cookbook*.

2 Tablespoons butter
1 cup less 2 Tablespoons sugar
6 eggs
1 pint plus 2 Tablespoons milk
piinch salt
1 unbaked 9 inch pastry pie crust

Cream butter, sugar and salt with electric mixer at medium speed. Add three eggs and beat for one minute, increase to high speed and add the other three eggs and beat three more minutes. Remove from mixer and add milk. Pour into pie crust and bake at 450° degrees for 10 minutes, then reduce to 325° and bake 25 minutes more.

FORGOTTEN PIE

In *Treasured Recipes from Angie Grant Elementary PTO* (1988), fifth grade teacher Mrs. Pryor shares this simple recipe that calls for you to leave your pie alone to think about cooking itself.

5 egg whites
1 1/2 cups
1/4 teaspoon salt
1/4 teaspoon cream of tartar
1 teaspoon vanilla
1 unbaked 9 inch pastry crust

Heat oven to 450°. Beat eggs til foamy. Add salt and cream of tartar to whites and beat until very stiff. Add sugar, 1 teaspoon at a time. Add vanilla. Pour into crust. Put into the oven and turn off as soon as you close the door. Forget about it and leave it overnight. Serve with ice cream or whipped cream and fresh berries.

HONEY SWEET POTATO PIE

This traditional version appears in the 1991 cookbook *Carnegie Public Library Cookbook II*, produced by the Eureka Springs Carnegie Public Library. It was contributed by Darlene Schrum.

1-3/4 cups sweet potatoes
1-1/2 cups milk
2 large eggs
1 cup honey or 1-1/4 cup sugar
1 teaspoon salt
1 teaspoon cinnamon
1/2 teaspoon nutmeg
1/2 teaspoon ginger
1 Tablespoon melted butter
1 whole wheat pastry pie crust

Preheat oven to 425°. Place all ingredients except pie shell in blender. Blend until smooth. Pour into pie shell. Bake until center is firm, 45-55 minutes (shield pie edges first 30 minutes). Delicious served warm or cold.

SWEET SOUTH'S KEY LIME PIE

Jacquelyn Henley has brought more than a quarter century's experience in home kitchens to the commercial scene, opening up Sweet South Diner and Bakery in Harrisburg, along Crowley's Ridge. Sandwiches and plate lunches during the week and breakfast all day on the weekends bring people for a first bite - but it's the extraordinary cakes and pies that keep them coming back.

2-14 ounce cans sweetened condensed milk
8 egg yolks
3/4 cup key lime juice
1/2 teaspoon vanilla extract
1 prepared 9 inch graham cracker crust

Heat oven to 350°. Mix milk, egg yolks, juice and extract. Pour into crust. Bake 20-25 minutes until center is completely set. Refrigerate 3-4 hours or overnight. Garnish with whipped cream, lime wedges and/or lime zest.

Chess and Custard Pies

BILL CLINTON'S FAVORITE LEMON CHESS PIE

In *Thirty Years At The Mansion: Recipes and Recollections by Liza Ashley (as told to Carolyn Huber)*, Chef Ashley shares stories and dishes from her three decades serving a succession of Arkansas's governors and their families, with anecdotes and details about what it was like over those years. The book, published in 1993, is full of delights from the kitchen at the Arkansas Governor's Mansion, including this lemon chess pie she says was former Arkansas governor (and United States President) Bill Clinton's absolute favorite.

1 unbaked 9 inch pastry pie crust
2 cups sugar
1/2 cup butter
5 eggs
1 cup milk
1 Tablespoon flour
1 Tablespoon cornmeal
1/4 cup fresh lemon juice
Grated rind of three lemons

Cream sugar and butter; add eggs and milk. Beat well. Add flour, cornmeal, lemon juice and lemon rind and stir until thoroughly incorporated. Pour mixture into pie shell. Bake at 350° for 35-40 minutes.

There may be a little wiggle in the custard when it is done. It will set up while cooling. Don't be worried if there's a sheen of melted butter on top when you remove it from the oven.

LEMON CHESS PIE

Miss Eloise Rhode contributed this recipe, which her mom wrote down in 1971, to *A Dash of This, A Pinch of That*. The filling of this pie is almost translucent - something I discovered when teaching a class on how to make it, and an errant sunbeam struck the glass pie pan and shone brightly through. Gorgeous and VERY lemony..

Crust
1 cup flour
1/2 cup shortening
1/2 teaspoon salt
few Tablespoons ice water

Filling
2 cups sugar
1 stick butter
4 eggs (add one at a time)
1/2 cup lemon juice
1 rounded Tablespoon flour

Mix flour, shortening and salt thoroughly. Add just enough ice water to be able to roll out a 9" crust. Lay crust across pan and refrigerate.

Beat all filling ingredients together until smooth. Pour into unbaked pie crust. Bake at 400° a few minutes, then turn down to 350°F and bake until firm.

MAPLE CREAM PIE

Elizabeth McMullen offered many delicious and unique pies at her Park Hill eatery, E's Bistro, over the years. Though the restaurant's time is over, she has graciously shared several of her recipes, including this smooth and delectable maple cream pie.

1 deep dish pie crust (frozen or handmade)

Bake at 350° for 10-12 minutes until lightly browned. Cool.

2 cups heavy whipping cream
3/4 cup sugar
4 Tablespoons cornstarch
4 Tablespoons unsalted butter

1/4 cup pure maple syrup
1 teaspoon maple extract
1 teaspoon vanilla extract
1/4 teaspoon salt

Heat cream and butter in saucepan together until butter is melted. Whisk in cornstarch and sugar, stirring continuously until thickened, 6-7 minutes. Stir syrup, extracts and salt into cream mixture. Pour into baked pie shell. Drizzle with melted butter.

4 Tablespoons unsalted butter, melted

3 Tablespoons sugar
1 1/2 teaspoons cinnamon

Mix melted butter, sugar and cinnamon and sprinkle over pie. Bake at 325° for 25-30 minutes or until crust is golden brown. Remove from oven. Let cool, then refrigerate until set, 2-3 hours. Serve with whipped cream.

MOTHER McQUAY'S ORANGE PIE

An unusual, fluffy pie for a nice change of pace. This recipe comes from the Sager Creek Quilts and Tea Room - the latter of which has since become history, though Sager Creek Quilts is still going very strong. It dates to 2003.

3 eggs
1-1/2 cups sugar
4 Tablespoons flour
4-1/2 Tablespoons butter
Juice of 2-3 large oranges

1 grated orange rind (~1/2 cup)
3/4 can evaporated milk
3/4 cup water
3/4 teaspoon salt
1 unbaked 9 inch pastry pie shell

Cream butter, sugar and flour. Add egg yolks, rind, and orange juice. Mix milk and water and add. Beat egg whites stiff and fold into mixture. Pour into pie shell and bake at 375° for 40-45 minutes until done. Will rise up high and be firm to the touch.

PEACH CUSTARD PIE

This version of the classic comes from the *War Eagle Mill Whole Grain Cookbook* by Zoe Medlin, who served as "milleress" at the facility from when it was first restored in 1973.

1/2 cup butter
2 cups whole wheat flour
1/4 teaspoon baking powder
1/2 teaspoon salt
1 cup brown sugar
1 teaspoon cinnamon
1 cup heavy cream
1 quart canned peaches
   or 2 packages frozen peaches
2 egg yolks, beaten

Cut butter into flour, baking powder, salt and 2 Tablespoons of the brown sugar until it looks like coarse meal. Press firmly into medium sized baking pan.

Arrange peaches on the surface to cover. Sprinkle fruit with mixture of cinnamon and remaining sugar. Bake 15 minutes at 350°. Beat egg yolks together with cream and pour over the top. Bake another 40 minutes.

PEANUT BUTTER BANANA PIE

This recipe comes from *Arkansas Heritage: Recipes Past and Present*, published in 1992 by the American Cancer Society, Arkansas Division.

1 baked 9 inch pastry pie crust
  in deep dish pan
1/2 cup peanut butter
1 cup confectioners' sugar
3 egg yolks, beaten
2/3 cups sugar
1/4 cup cornstarch
1/8 teaspoon salt
2 cups milk, scalded
2 Tablespoons butter
1/2 teaspoon vanilla extract
2 bananas, sliced
3 egg whites, stiffly beaten

Cut peanut butter into confectioners' sugar in bowl until crumbly. Sprinkle into pie shell. Combine egg yolks, sugar, cornstarch and salt in bowl; beat well. Heat milk in double boiler. Add a small amount of hot milk to egg mixture. Add egg mixture to double boiler. Cook over hot water until thickened, stirring constantly. Remove from heat. Stir in butter and vanilla. Place banana slices over crumbly mixture in pie shell. Pour in cooked mixture. Spread stiffly beaten egg whites over top, sealing to edge. Bake at 350° for five minutes, or until meringue begins to brown.

Chess and Custard Pies

PEANUT BUTTER CUSTARD PIE

It would be hard to beat the simplicity of this recipe from *Feed My Sheep*, the 1987 Second Baptist Church cookbook. Simple ingredients and simple directions make a great pie that travels well. Perfect with milk.

3 eggs	1 cup light corn syrup
2/3 cup sugar	3/4 cup peanut butter
1/2 teaspoon salt	1 unbaked 9 inch pastry or
1/2 cup butter, melted	graham cracker pie crust

Mix first six ingredients together. Pour into pie crust. Bake until set and brown, 375° for 45 minutes.

PEANUT BUTTER PIE

Mrs. Oscar Pearcy

5 tbsp peanut butter   1 tsp vanilla
1 cup sugar   2 egg yolks
                1 cup milk

Mix peanut butter, sugar, milk and eggs. Cook until thick. Add vanilla and cook until creamy. Put in cooked pie shell and put on meringue and brown.

* * * * * * * *

PINTO BEAN PIE

Now hear me out - this pie is far better than it sounds. Putting pinto beans and coconut into a pie might seem an odd combination, but it works. On the surface, it appears it might have roots with the navy bean pie - an alternative to soul food dishes such as sweet potato pie that contained ingredients deemed inappropriate by Wallace Faud Muhammad, a restaurateur in the 1910s and 20s before founding the Nation of Islam in the 1930s. However, pinto bean pie is far more likely to be a subsistence pie, where the soft pinto bean replaces another starch that might have been unavailable.

This recipe originally called for mashing the beans I took a half-and-half method with this and left half the beans whole. The result is a flavor very reminiscent of a peanut patty.

1/2 cup cooked and mashed pinto beans
1-1/2 cup sugar
1 stick butter
2 eggs
1 cup coconut
1 teaspoon vanilla
1 unbaked 9 inch pastry pie shell

Mix and fill pie shell. Bake at 350° for 30 minutes. Top with whipped cream if desired.

PINEAPPLE CREAM CHEESE PIE

Unlike most cream cheese pies, this one is baked, and the fruit comes out on the bottom for a filling, tangy and sweet pie. This recipe comes from Bernica Haley.

Pineapple layer
1/3 cup sugar
8 ounces crushed pineapple with juice
1 Tablespoon cornstarch

Cream cheese layer
1 - 8 ounce block cream cheese at room temperature
1/2 cup sugar
2 eggs
1/2 teaspoon vanilla
1/4 cup chopped pecans
1 teaspoon salt
1/2 cup milk

1 unbaked 9 inch pie crust

Combine sugar, cornstarch and pineapple in juice in a small saucepan. Cook over medium heat, simmering until thick and translucent. Remove from heat; set aside to cool.

Blend cream cheese, sugar and salt. Add eggs, one at a time, beating two minutes after each addition. Blend in milk and vanilla.

Spread cooled pineapple layer over pie crust. Pour cream cheese mixture over. Sprinkle on pecans. Bake at 400° for 10 minutes, then reduce to 325° and bake 50 minutes more.

PUMPKIN PIE

Pumpkins have been part of the diet for Arkansas for centuries. Long before European settlers came here, Native Americans were growing them as a foodstuff - even before maize and beans. There are records of more recent times where the seeds were removed from the fruit (yes, pumpkin is a fruit, though often called a vegetable) and filled with honey, milk, and spices such as sumac and baked directly on coals. The gourd, which gets its name from "pepon," the Greek word for "large melon," is cited as being used in pies back to 1570, where Bartolomeo Scappi recorded a recipe of pie blended with soft white cheeses like ricotta to make a proto-pumpkin cheesecake in his book *Opera dell'arte del cucinare*. Francois Pierre la Varenne in 1651 shared his take on the dish in *Le Vrai Cuisinier Francois* (The True French Cookbook) as being pureed pumpkin with ground almonds, butter, and milk baked in a pastry shell. Amelia Simmons included pumpkin puddings, very similar to our modern pumpkin pies, in the first American cookbook, *American Cookery by an American Orphan*, in 1796.

There's nothing quite like a good old fashioned pumpkin pie. This deep dish version actually goes by the name Thanksgiving Pumpkin Pie and is accredited to Cleva and Charlie Smith. An identical recipe appears in *Recipes from Arkansas* by the Arkansas School Food Service Association. If you don't have a deep dish pie plate, go ahead and spread this into two separate pastry pie crusts in regular or slightly smaller dishes (8 inch works great). This will prevent an uneven pie. I also like to use the method of splitting your pie dough, rolling it translucent thin, laying in one layer and dotting it with butter before laying a second layer on, to provide a crispier crust for this dense, heavy pie.

1 can (2 cups) pumpkin puree
1 - 14 ounce can sweetened condensed milk
2 eggs
1 cup sugar
1 teaspoon ground cinnamon
1/2 teaspoon ground ginger
1/2 teaspoon ground nutmeg
1/2 teaspoon salt
1 unbaked deep dish pastry pie crust

Preheat oven to 425°. With wire whisk, beat pumpkin and all other ingredients. Pour into unbaked pie shell. Bake 15 minutes. Reduce heat to 350°; continue baking 35 to 40 minutes or until knife inserted 1 inch from center comes out clean. Cool. Garnish if desired.

Chess and Custard Pies

157

PUMPKIN PRALINE PIE

Viv Barnhill makes pies just about every day - not just for Ms. Lena's Pie Shop but for her family, too. This is a gorgeous favorite.

1 - 15 ounce can pumpkin puree (not pumpkin pie filling)
3/4 cup packed dark brown sugar
2 teaspoons ground cinnamon
1 teaspoon ground ginger
1/2 teaspoon ground nutmeg
1/2 teaspoon salt
1/4 teaspoon ground cloves
1 cup evaporated milk
3 eggs
2 teaspoons vanilla extract

Topping
1 cup pecans, finely chopped
1/2 cup packed dark brown sugar
1/8 teaspoon salt
1 Tablespoon dark Karo syrup
1 teaspoon vanilla extract
1 Tablespoon granulated sugar

1 unbaked 9 inch pastry pie crust

Add pumpkin, brown sugar, spices, and salt to a medium saucepan and whisk to combine. Cook over medium-high heat 4 minutes, stirring constantly. Remove from heat and whisk in evaporated milk, followed by eggs and vanilla. Pour filling into pie crust. Bake at 350° for 40-50 minutes, until pie is cracked around the edges and the center barely jiggles.

While pie is baking, add pecans, brown sugar, and salt to bowl and stir until evenly combined. Add corn syrup and vanilla and mix until evenly moistened. Sprinkle topping evenly over pie, then dust with sugar. Cover edges of pie with foil and return to oven for another 20 minutes or until toothpick inserted in center comes out clean.

PUMPKIN PIE x 7

Another large batch pie recipe from The Purple Cow's collection - Todd Gold shares how to make seven pumpkin pies at once.

Crust
7 unbaked 9 inch pastry pie shells
12 ounces apricot preserves

Filling
3-3/4 cups sugar
1/3 cup (packed) golden brown sugar
1/3 cup cornstarch
3 Tablespoons cinnamon
4 teaspoons ground ginger
1 teaspoon nutmeg
1 and a half teaspoons salt
5 - 15 oz cans solid pack pumpkin (not pumpkin pie filling)
2 cups heavy whipping cream
1 3/4 cups milk
2 cups sour cream
16 eggs, slightly beaten
1 and a half Tablespoons vanilla extract
3 Tablespoons molasses

Heat oven to 425°. Allow pie crusts to sit at room temperature for 14 minutes. Using a fork, prick the crust on sides and bottoms of each pie plate. Bake for 15-18 minutes.

After 10 minutes, check to see that crust is not sliding down into pan - if so, push up with your fingers or a spatula. Allow to cool.

Puree preserves just enough to remove lumps, then spread over bottoms and sides of each pie crust. Set aside.

Set oven to 350°. Stir first seven ingredients of filling together until mixture is uniform. Add remaining ingredients and whisk until uniformly blended.

Divide filling among the seven pie shells and bake for approximately 60 minutes. Test with sharp point of a paring knife. If done, should come out clean. Cool completely then refrigerate.

Serve garnished with whipped cream.

PUMPKIN PRALINE PIE

Louise Russom contributed this recipe to *Seasoned with Love*, the Markham United Methodist Church cookbook. It's very moist and flavorful.

1 unbaked 9 inch pie crust
1/2 cup finely chopped pecans
2 Tablespoons butter
1/3 cup + 2/3 cup brown sugar
2 eggs
1-16 ounce can pumpkin
1 teaspoon cinnamon
1/2 teaspoon salt
1-12 ounce can evaporated milk
1 teaspoon vanilla

Blend pecans, butter and 1/3 cup brown sugar and press gently into bottom of pie shell.

Heat oven to 450°. Beat eggs until frothy. Add remaining ingredients one at a time until well mixed. Pour over praline layer. Bake 10 minutes, then reduce heat to 350° and bake an additional 40-50 minutes.

SOY SWEET POTATO PIE

This recipe from the Arkansas Soybean Promotion Board utilizes soymilk instead of dairy for a dairy-free sweet potato pie option.

3/4 cup granulated sugar
1 teaspoon ground cinnamon
1/2 teaspoon salt
1/2 teaspoon ground ginger
1/4 teaspoon ground cloves
2 large eggs
1 and 3/4 cup cooked and mashed sweet potatoes
12 ounces soymilk
1 unbaked 9 inch deep dish pastry pie crust
Cool Whip whipped topping (optional)

Mix sugar, cinnamon, salt, ginger and cloves in a small bowl. In a separate, larger bowl, beat the eggs. Stir in the sweet potatoes and sugar-spice mixture, then gradually stir in the soymilk.

Pour the mixture into the unbaked pie shell and bake in a pre-heated oven at 425° for 15 minutes. Reduce the temperature to 350° and bake another 40-50 minutes, or until a knife inserted near the center comes out clean. Cool on a wire rack for two hours.

Serve immediately or refrigerate. Top with whipped cream before serving.

MS. LENA'S SQUASH PIE

A recipe from my very first book, *Arkansas Pie: A Delicious Slice of The Natural State*, submitted by Viv Barnhill, from her mom Lena, who was the original pie shop maven at the Highway 33 spot in De Valls Bluff.

2 eggs
2 cups milk
3/4 cup sugar
1 cup cooked squash
1/2 teaspoon salt
1/2 teaspoon pumpkin pie spice
1/2 teaspoon vanilla
1 unbaked 9 inch pastry pie crust

Blend all ingredients. Pour into pre-baked pie shell and bake at 375° degrees for 30 minutes or until knife comes out clean.

BUBBA's SWEET POTATO PIE

I miss my dear sweet friends Sharon Woodson and Anne Wood. Sharon created the incredible Honey Pies in Little Rock, and she and Anne blossomed some of the most amazing pies to ever bloom in our market. Though they have moved along to other adventures, the bakery (now called Blue Cake Honey Pies after a semi-merger with reputed cake place Blue Cake Company), you can still order one of these magnificent creamy pies - or make one yourself!

For this recipe, ready frozen mashed or canned sweet potatoes work great. If you'd like your filling extra silky, just run it through a blender or food processor before starting.

2 egg whites
1/8 teaspoon salt
2 egg yolks
1-1/2 cups mashed sweet potato
1/2 teaspoon vanilla
1/2 cup granulated sugar

1/2 teaspoon allspice
1/4 teaspoon cinnamon
2 Tablespoons melted butter
3/4 cup whole milk or evaporated milk
1 prepared 9 inch pastry pie crust

Whip egg whites and salt until stiff peaks form.

In second bowl or your blender or food processor, incorporate: yolks, sweet potato, vanilla, sugar, spices and melted butter. Once fully mixed, add milk. Finally, gently fold in the egg whites. Lay into pie pan. Bake at 375° for 30 minutes, covering pie crust edges if necessary, then at 350° for an additional 30 or until the center is set.

DORA MAY PEARSON'S SWEET POTATO PIE

This recipe is from David Franks, and includes a spicy gingerbread crust.

Crust
1-3/4 cup crushed gingersnaps
2 Tablespoons dark brown sugar
1/4 cup melted butter

Filling
3 eggs
1 cup brown sugar
2 Tablespoons melted butter
1/4 cup lemon juice

1 teaspoon cinnamon
1/2 teaspoon ginger
1/2 teaspoon nutmeg
1 and a half cups cooked, mashed sweet potato
1 cup milk
1 gingersnap pie crust or unbaked 9 inch pastry pie crust

Heat oven to 425°. Mix all crust ingredients together. Press into 9" pie pan; even out by pressing with second pie pan. Bake 10-15 minutes. Watch carefully for burning. Cool, then refrigerate for an hour. Brush with egg white before filling.

Heat oven to 375°. Beat eggs; beat in remaining ingredients in order. Pour into crust; bake until center is done, 50-60 minutes.

SWEET POTATO PIE

The excellent *Sampling Arkansas*, the 1983 cookbook by the Arkansas Division of the American Cancer Society, contains quite a few winning pie recipes. I found particular joy with this version by Mrs. Paul Farrell of the Monroe Unit in Brinkley.

Filling
1-1/2 cups mashed sweet potatoes
3/4 cups sugar
3 whole eggs, well beaten
7/8 cup half-and-half
 or evaporated milk

1 unbaked 9 inch pastry pie crust

Topping
1/4 cup butter
1/2 cup brown sugar
3/4 cup chopped pecans

Combine all filling ingredients in large bowl and pour into pie shell. Bake at 375° for 25 minutes. Remove carefully from oven and sprinkle on topping. Return to oven and bake another 25-30 minutes more until set. Reduce heat to 350° if topping seems to be browning too quickly, or cover with foil.

The Great Arkansas Pie Book

IRMA'S SWEET POTATO PIE

D.L. Lindsey opened Lindsey's Hospitality House in 1956. Today, his son Donnie Lindsey, Jr. and Donnie's wife Eleanor continue to serve up extraordinary smoked and fried chicken, lunch plates, barbecue, and this craveable sweet potato pie.

1 pound sweet potato
1/2 cup butter, softened
1 cup white sugar
1/2 cup evaporated milk
2 eggs
1/2 teaspoon nutmeg
1/2 teaspoon cinnamon
1 teaspoon pure vanilla extract
1 unbaked 9 inch pastry pie crust

Boil sweet potato whole in skin for 40-50 minutes, or until done. Rinse cold water over the sweet potato, and remove the skin.

Break apart sweet potato in bowl. Add butter and mix well. Stir in sugar, milk, eggs, nutmeg, cinnamon and vanilla. Beat on medium speed until mixture is smooth. Pour filling into an unbaked pie crust.

Bake at 350° for 55-60 minutes, or until knife inserted in center comes out clean. Pie will puff up, and sink down as it cools.

Chess and Custard Pies

SAY IT AIN'T SAY'S SWEET POTATO PIE

This pie recipe from Derotha McIntosh has circulated a bit. It's garnered much fame because of its creator, Robert "Say" McIntosh, known as the Sweet Potato Pie King. The community activist and restaurateur, who passed away in June 2023, may be best known for this remarkable pie.

Pastry
- 1-1/2 cups all-purpose flour
- 1/2 teaspoon salt
- 6 Tablespoons vegetable shortening
  or 3 tablespoons unsalted butter or margarine, chilled
- 4-5 tablespoons ice water

Filling
- 1-1/2 cup mashed, cooked sweet potatoes or yams
- 3/4 cup packed light-brown sugar
- 1 teaspoon ground cinnamon
- 1/2 teaspoon ground nutmeg
- 1/2 teaspoon ground allspice
- 3 eggs
- 1-3/4 cups condensed milk
- 1 Tablespoon butter or margarine, melted

In a medium bowl, blend flour and salt. Use a pastry cutter or two knives to cut in shortening, butter or margarine, until mixture resembles coarse crumbs. Sprinkle with ice water, a tablespoon at a time, and toss lightly with a fork until the mixture begins to bind. Gather dough into a ball, flatten into a fat disk, cover and refrigerate for about 30 minutes.

Roll out refrigerated dough on a lightly floured surface into a 12-inch circle. Fold dough over rolling pin and lay into pie plate. Trim edges to 1 inch beyond rim. Fold edge under and crimp or flute.

Heat over to 400°. In a medium bowl, combine sweet potatoes, brown sugar, cinnamon, nutmeg and allspice. In another medium bowl, beat eggs; stir in condensed milk and butter or margarine until blended. Stir into sweet potato mixture. Pour filling into pastry-lined pie plate. Bake 45 minutes or until filling is set. Cool on a wire rack. Serve warm or cold.

SINFULLY SWEET SWEET POTATO PIE

This remarkable three layer pie won Kelli Marks not only the Say It Ain't Say's Sweet Potato Pie Contest at the Mosaic Templars Cultural Center, it also won her due notice as a maker of pies. From bottom to top, purple sweet potato custard, a lighter purple cheesecake, and a delightful whipped top, make this one memorable pie for the ages. Though I included it in *Another Slice of Arkansas Pie*, it's too good not to share again. Be sure to use sweet potatoes with purple flesh.

Crust

3-1/2 cups all-purpose flour
1/2 cup melted butter
1/2 cup shortening
5 Tablespoons vodka
 (can sub water)
2 egg yolks
2 Tablespoons. lemon juice
1 teaspoon salt
1 Tablespoon. sugar
1/4 cup ground toasted pecans

Combine flour, sugar, salt, and shortening in to bowl of stand mixer. Mix until small chunks of shortening are seen. Add egg yolks while mixing, followed by lemon juice, vodka, lemon juice and melted butter. Mix until crust comes together in a ball.

Roll out between two layers of plastic wrap. Once the desired thickness, sprinkle pecans over the crust. Roll crust once more to push pecans into the crust. Use the bottom layer of plastic wrap to pick up the crust and turn it into the pie tin.

Filling

Purple sweet potatoes
 (enough for 1-1/2 cups)
A little honey
Sea salt
1/2 cup granulated sugar
1/2 cup brown sugar
2 eggs
6 Tablespoons butter, melted
1 teaspoon vanilla
1/4 teaspoon salt
1/4 teaspoon cinnamon
1/8 teaspoon ginger
1/2 teaspoon allspice
2 Tablespoons bourbon
1/2 cup heavy cream
1-1/2 teaspoon cornstarch

Peel sweet potatoes. Cube potatoes into about 1/2-inch pieces and lay out on a sheet pan. Drizzle with a small amount of honey and sprinkle with sea salt. Roast until potatoes are soft to the touch, about 30 minutes.

Place all ingredients into a blender. Blend on high until no lumps remain. If color is not as purple as you'd like, add a few tablespoons of ube powder (needed for cheesecake layer) or

Chess and Custard Pies

add a few drops purple food color. Pour into unbaked crust. Bake at 350° for 30 minutes. Cover edges of crust with aluminum foil to keep crust from getting too brown. While baking, make cheesecake layer. It will be added on top of this and baked again. Make sure to leave room for it.

Cheesecake layer
8 ounces cream cheese
1/4 cup granulated sugar
1 egg
1/4 cup sour cream
1/4 cup whipping cream
2 Tablespoons. ube powder
(available at Asian food stores)

Beat cream cheese until soft, add sugar until combined, add sour cream and egg. Finish with whipping cream and ube powder. If a deeper color is desired, add another tablespoon of ube powder or a few drops of purple food color. Pour on top of pie and bake for another 20 minutes.

Topping
5 ounces heavy cream (by weight)
3 ounces granulated sugar (by weight)
8 ounce block cream cheese
1 teaspoon cinnamon
1/2 teaspoon nutmeg
1/4 teaspoon salt
1 teaspoon vanilla

Whip heavy cream and sugar on medium until peaks begin to form. Add cold cream cheese a tablespoon at a time until incorporated. Scrape bowl, add cinnamon, nutmeg, salt, and vanilla, beat about 1 minute longer until no big lumps are visible. Spread or pipe on the top of the cooled pie.

Pumpkin Pie

3/4 cups brown sugar
1 tablespoon flour
1/2 teaspoon salt
1/2 teaspoon cinnamon
1/4 "   nutmeg
1/4 "   ginger
1 1/2 cups canned or cooked pumpkin
1 1/2 cups canned milk
1 egg well beaten

mix all ingredients together & beat thoroughly until smooth. pour into deep pie lined with unbaked pastry bake in hot oven (450°F) 10 minutes. reduce to slow oven (325°F) bake 30 min or until firm. makes one pie.

ARKANSAS POSSUM PIE

I've been fortunate enough to watch Tusk and Trotter grow since it originally opened in 2011. Chef Rob Nelson has continued to grow a community of local producers, farmers, brewers and such to feed into the duplexed dining rooms and to hungry patrons who are seeking not only locally produced food but cuisine with a story - an Ozark story. It's no surprise, then, to find Arkansas Possum Pie on the menu. This is a pie both so tasty and such a good representative of this dessert found all over the state, that *People Magazine* named it the best pie in Arkansas. This recipe makes 8-10 servings or, I discovered, one 9x13" pan.

Pecan shortbread crust
4 cups flour
2 cups butter, melted
1 cup brown sugar
3 cups pecans, chopped
1 teaspoon cornstarch

Cream cheese layer
3 - 8 ounce blocks cream cheese
1 and a half cups powdered sugar
6 Tablespoons heavy cream
1 Tablespoon vanilla extract
1/4 cup honey

Heat oven to 350°. Combine all crust ingredients in a bowl and mix. Place 1 cup in each mold, enough to make 1/4 inch crust on bottom and sides. Bake for 20 minutes, rotating halfway.

Whip all cream cheese layer ingredients in a Kitchenaid machine with paddle attachment until light and fluffy. Scoop into molds evenly.

Chocolate layer
3 cups sugar
1 cup cocoa powder
9 Tablespoons cornstarch
4 Tablespoons flour
1 teaspoon salt
9 egg yolks
6 cups milk
6 Tablespoons butter

Whipped topping
2 cups heavy cream
1 cup powdered sugar
1 teaspoon 4 Roses bourbon

For chocolate layer, combine sugar, cocoa, cornstarch, flour and salt in a saucepan and whisk until there are no lumps. In a separate bowl, whisk egg yolks and milk, then pour mixture over dry mix. Whisk until smooth. Place over medium heat while whisking until nice and thick. Remove from heat and stir in butter and bourbon. Let cool, then spoon over cream cheese layer. Chill.

Whip all the topping ingredients together. Pour into a whipped cream dispenser. Garnish pies with this cream and serve.

Chocolate Pies

BASIC CHOCOLATE PIE

Simple yet effective, good with either cream or meringue on top or served with ice cream - this basic chocolate pie recipe is a sturdy winner.

2 cups sugar	3 Tablespoons butter
3 heaping Tablespoons flour	1 teaspoon vanilla
3 heaping Tablespoons cocoa	3 egg yolks
3 cups half-and-half or milk	1 baked pastry pie shell

In saucepan over medium heat, bring together sugar, flour, cocoa and half-and-half and stir until thickened. Whip egg yolks until creamy. Drop a tablespoon of the hot chocolate mixture into the yolks and stir to temper, then pour yolks into chocolate. Add butter and vanilla. Remove from heat and allow to cool for 20 minutes.

Heat oven to 350°. Pour mixture into pastry pie shell. If using meringue, place on top. Bake 10 minutes. Allow to cool completely before serving.

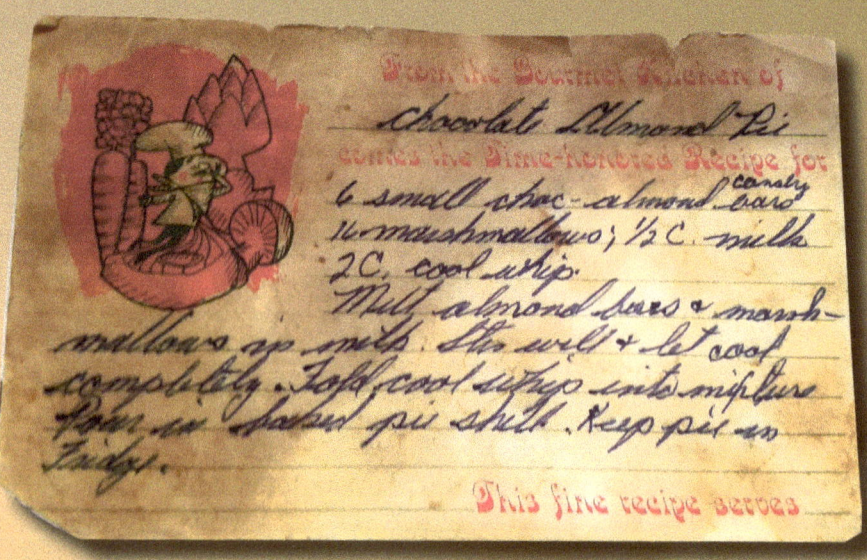

From the Gourmet Kitchen of Chocolate Almond Pie comes the Time-honored Recipe for

6 small choc-almond candy bars
16 marshmallows; 1/2 C. milk
2 C. cool whip.

Melt almond bars & marshmallows in milk. Stir well & let cool completely. Fold cool whip into mixture. Pour in baked pie shell. Keep pie in fridge.

This fine recipe serves

This recipe is from the collection of Evelyn Weldon.

Chocolate Pies

BITTERSWEET PIE

This cream pie comes from *Arkansas Cooking 1836-1986: Sesquicentennial Souvenir Cookbook* published by the Arkansas State Employees Association in 1985. The original recipe was submitted by Daisy V. Briscoe, who worked at Arkansas Tech University. I have added some instructions.

- 1 cup milk
- 20 marshmallows *or* 45 mini-marshmallows
- 1/4 teaspoon salt
- 1/2 teaspoon almond flavoring
- 1 cup heavy whipping cream
- 1/2 cup unsweetened chocolate, grated
- 1 baked 9 inch pastry pie shell

Heat milk and marshmallows in a sauce pot until marshmallows are dissolved. Add salt and almond flavoring; chill.

Whip the cream until peaks form. Set aside 2 tablespoons chocolate. Fold cream and chocolate into marshmallow mixture and turn into pie shell. Garnish with remaining chocolate. Chill for several hours in refrigerator before serving. You may garnish with additional whipped cream.

While you can substitute 1 1/4 cups non-dairy whipped topping for the cream, it does change the texture somewhat.

BLACK BOTTOM PIE

For a long time, I wondered why The Colonial Steak House in Pine Bluff was the only restaurant in the state to consistently offer this classic favorite on its menu. Then I started making them myself and I understood. This is a complex pie, but oh so worth it. The chocolate layer under the rum custard is how the pie got its name.

Crust
1 and a quarter cups graham cracker crumbs
1 Tablespoon confectioners sugar
1 teaspoon cinnamon
1/4 cup melted butter

Topping
1 cup heavy cream
1 Tablespoon sugar
chocolate for garnish

Filling
1 envelope (1 Tablespoon) unflavored gelatin
1/4 cup cold water
1 cup sugar
1 Tablespoon cornstarch
dash salt
1-3/4 cups milk, scalded
4 eggs, separated
3 Tablespoons dark rum
2 ounces semi-sweet chocolate
1 teaspoon vanilla
1/8 teaspoon cream of tartar

Chocolate Pies

Combine crust ingredients and press into 9 inch pie plate. Set aside.

Dissolve gelatin in water; set aside.

Combine half the sugar with cornstarch and salt. Stir into scalded milk. Beat egg yolks in top of double boiler; gradually whisk in hot milk mixture. Continue to cook over simmering water 10 minutes or until crust thickens. Remove one cup of the custard. Mix softened gelatin and rum into remaining custard and stir to dissolve. Remove from heat.

Combine reserved custard with chocolate and vanilla; whisk smooth. While still hot, spread over bottom of prepared crust. Chill.

Beat egg whites with cream of tartar until foamy. Gradually add remaining sugar and beat until soft peaks form. Fold rum custard into egg whites. Pour over chocolate layer in pan. Chill.

Beat together heavy cream with sugar until peaks are shiny. Turn out onto top of pie, spreading from center to edges. Shave chocolate over top. Chill until ready to serve.

CHOCOLATE CHESS PIE

One of Alma French's recipes from her days at Ed and Alma's in Benton - while it may not bear the fame of the Mile High Pies, it's certainly a winner.

1/4 cup melted butter
1 cup sugar
3 and a half Tablespoons cocoa
1/8 teaspoon salt
2 eggs, beaten
1 can evaporated milk
1 unbaked 9 inch pastry pie crust
2 teaspoons vanilla
3/4 cup chopped pecans
whipped cream

In mixing bowl mix butter, sugar, cocoa, and salt until well combined. Add eggs; beat by hand or on medium speed for two minutes. Stir in milk and vanilla. Fold in pecans.

Pour mixture into pie shell. Bake at 350° for 45 minutes or until inserted knife comes out clean. Cool on rack. Pipe whipped cream around edges. Serve warm or cold.

CHOCOLATE CHESS PIE

I have in my notes that this is the recipe for chocolate chess pie like at Alley-Oop's, a longtime west Little Rock restaurant known for this pie and its traditional chess pie cousin. I know I've photographed the pie a dozen times for not just my books but for Food Network, Serious Eats and a number of other publications - but whether or not this is the same recipe Gary Duke has shared in the past, well, I'm not for certain. It's good, though.

1 and a half cups sugar
3 Tablespoons cocoa
3 beaten eggs
5 Tablespoons evaporated milk
2 teaspoons apple cider vinegar
1 Tablespoon vanilla extract
4 Tablespoons melted butter
1 baked 9 inch pastry pie crust

Sift together sugar and cocoa. Beat together eggs, milk, vinegar, vanilla and butter. Add sugar and cocoa and incorporate.

Pour into pie crust and bake at 350° for 35 minutes or until surface begins to form bubbly pits and is firm. Serve with ice cream or whipped cream.

Chocolate Pies

CHOCOLATE CHESS PIE

Luby's, the famed Texas cafeteria chain, used to have a location right here in Little Rock, a couple miles down Markham from my personal abode. This is the franchise's famed chocolate chess pie recipe.

1 and a half cups sugar
1/2 cup all-purpose flour
1/2 cup butter
2 teaspoons unsweetened cocoa
3 extra large eggs or 4 large eggs
1-1/4 cups evaporated milk
1/4 cup light corn syrup
1 ounce German baking chocolate, melted
2 teaspoons vanilla
1 unbaked 9-inch pie shell

Heat oven to 375°. In large bowl, combine flour, sugar, butter, and cocoa. Blend well. Add eggs, one at a time, mixing well after each addition. Add milk, corn syrup, chocolate, and vanilla. Mix well. Pour into pie shell. Bake 45-50 minutes or until toothpick inserted in center comes out *almost* clean. Do not overbake.

CHOCOLATE PIE

Anderson's Restaurant was for a long time the place to go for outstanding steaks and seafood in White County and surrounds. Frank Anderson opened Anderson's Grill at the intersections of US Highways 64 and 67 back in 1953. Though Frank passed away in 1957, his wife Margaret and son Bruce continued the operation, alongside the Bel Mar Motel, and expanded over the years. Bruce would go on to open Cajun's Wharf in Little Rock in 1974, followed by Shorty Smalls in 1980.

Though fresh Gulf Coast seafood and prime steaks were the main attractions, the pies became a great draw, with piemakers Alberta Plummer and Carrie Pruitt crafting fine versions of lemon meringue, coconut, egg custard (recipe on page 142) and chocolate pies. The restaurant burned in 1985, but these recipes live on.

Crust:
1/2 cup shortening
1/2 teaspoon salt
4 Tablespoons cold water
1 and a half cups all-purpose flour, divided

Filling:
3 eggs, divided
1 cup plus 6 Tablespoons granulated sugar, divided
3 Tablespoons unsweetened cocoa
1/4 teaspoon salt
2 cups milk
2 to 3 Tablespoons melted butter
4 Tablespoons all-purpose flour

To make the crust: Melt shortening in pan over low heat. Remove from heat. Add salt and water. Stir in 1 cup of the flour, then knead in the remaining half cup flour. Roll out pastry and fit loosely into a 10-inch pie pan. Bake at 400 degrees 10-12 minutes or until brown. Cool before filling.

To make the filling: Separate eggs, reserving whites for meringue. Beat egg yolks well. Add 3/8 cup of the sugar, the cocoa, salt, milk and butter. Heat until sugar dissolves. Mix flour with 5/8 cup sugar.

Blend into cooked cocoa mixture and cook, stirring constantly, until thick. Pour into baked, cooled crust. Cover with meringue made from 3 egg whites whipped with 6 tablespoons granulated sugar. Brown in oven at 350° to 375°.

CHOCOLATE ICE BOX PIE

This really, truly rich pie comes from the Markham United Methodist Church - now known as Faith United Methodist Church - which happens to be my local voting spot. It appears in the *Seasoned with Love* cookbook courtesy Doris Grimsley.

1 prepared 8 inch graham cracker pie crust
2 ounces unsweetened chocolate
1 can sweetened condensed milk
1/2 cup hot water
8 ounces heavy whipping cream
1/4 teaspoon salt, divided
1/2 teaspoon vanilla

Melt chocolate in top of double boiler. Add sweetened condensed milk and 1/8 teaspoon salt. Heat, stirring occasionally, until mixture will drop from a spoon (between four and eight minutes). Gradually stir in water, keeping mixture smooth, until thickened (up to five minutes. Pour into pastry shell. Cool on counter half an hour, then refrigerate at least three hours.

Beat heavy cream together with remaining salt and vanilla until fluffy. Top pie and refrigerate for at least one hour before serving.

Notes

Granny's Chocolate Pie

1 c sugar
2 T flour
2 T chocolate (silver serv. spoon)
1 C milk (1 small pet milk finish with sweet milk to make 1 C
4 eggs separated - add 1 at a time
Then add 2 more C of milk
When cooked add tab of butter
Vanilla flavoring

Crust
1 C plain flour
dash salt
3/4 C water
1/4 C shortening
mix flour & shortening until mealy
add ice water

Chocolate Pies

CHOCOLATE PIE

In the 1986 cookbook *Sunday Best* by Little Rock's Calvary Baptist Church, Joyce Nicholson shares this recipe that calls for an entire bag of chocolate chips. Yes, it IS chocolatey. And it absolutely cries out for heavy whipping cream.

1 package semi-sweet chocolate chips
4 eggs
3 Tablespoons sugar
4 Tablespoons milk
1/4 teaspoon vanilla
1 cup heavy whipping cream
1 baked 9 inch pastry pie crust
   (can also use graham crust)

Melt chocolate chips in saucepan. Separate eggs. Beat egg yolks together with milk and sugar. Combine with melted chocolate. Beat egg whites until stiff peaks form. Fold into chocolate mixture and lay into pie crust. Chill until set.

Beat whipping cream with vanilla until peaks form. Top pie and serve.

CHOCOLATE PEPPERMINT PIE

This recipe from the *Presbyterian Cookbook* produces a very light, almost foamy pie. It was contributed by Mrs. F.W. Kellogg

3 standard candy canes	1/2 cup heavy cream
2 cups milk	1 chocolate graham cracker crust
3 egg yolks, beaten	or
1 envelope gelatin	15 chocolate wafer cookies,
1/4 cup water	crushed
3 egg whites	plus 2 Tablespoons butter

If using chocolate wafers, combine with butter and press into 9 inch pie pan. Dissolve candy canes in milk overnight. Add to three yolks in double boiler over simmering water and cook until custard coats back of a spoon. Dissolve gelatin in water and stir into custard. Set aside.

Beat egg whites til foamy. Add cream and beat until peak stiffen. If the flavor is not strong enough, add a couple drops of peppermint extract. Pour into chocolate crust and chill for 3 to 4 hours.

FRENCH CHOCOLATE PIE

This recipe from one of the most popular Arkansas cookbooks ever published, *Little Rock Cooks*, is a time-tested and excellent chocolate dessert. The 1972 green comb-bound book compiled by the Junior League of Little Rock is also available in a traditionally published binding and has sold more than ten thousand copies. The recipe comes from Mrs. William R. Overton.

2 egg whites	1/2 cup sugar
1/8 teaspoon salt	1/2 teaspoon vanilla
1/8 teaspoon cream of tartar	1/2 cup pecans, chopped

Beat egg whites with salt and cream of tartar until foamy. Add sugar gradually, beating until very stiff. Fold in vanilla and nuts. Spread in a 9-inch pie pan which has been greased and floured. Bake for 50-55 minutes at 300°. Allow to cool completely.

1/2 cup butter or margarine	1 teaspoon vanilla
3/4 cup sugar	2 egg yolks
1-1/2 square unsweetened baking chocolate, melted and cooled	2 whole eggs
	1/2 pint cream, whipped

Cream butter. Gradually add sugar and blend in chocolate and vanilla. Beat with mixer at medium speed until smooth. Add yolks and whole eggs, one at a time. Beat four minutes after each addition, for a total of at least 15 minutes. Spread in cooled pie shell. Top with slightly sweetened whipped cream. Best served after several hours of refrigeration.

FUDGE CREAM PIE

Marlar's Cafeteria is one of those great local joints that folks outside a small radius of Magnolia might be missing out on. The traditional menu, the line with all those choices, the take-and-bake case, all hallmarks of a restaurant so good you have to have the grub now and later.

A few years ago, a Tie Dye Travels reader sent me this recipe, attributing it to Marlar's and piquing my curiosity. On my visit, I actually fell for a surprisingly good raisin pie - but this one's also a real winner.

1-1/3 cups + 6 Tablespoons sugar
1/4 cup all-purpose flour
1/4 cup cocoa powder
1 - 12 ounce can evaporated milk
3 egg yolks, lightly beaten
2 Tablespoons butter
2 teaspoons vanilla extract
1 baked 9 inch pastry pie shell
1/2 cup chopped nuts
3 egg whites
1/4 teaspoon cream of tartar

Sift together flour, cocoa. and all but six tablespons of the sugar and heat in a saucepan. Gradually stir in evaporated milk. Stir over medium heat until mixture comes to a boil and thickens. Reduce heat; stir four minutes. Add small amount of hot mixture to egg yolks to temper; return all to pan. Cook three minutes more or until mixture is very thick. Remove from heat; stir in butter and one and a half teaspoons vanilla. Cool five minutes; turn into prepared pie shell. Top with nuts.

Beat egg whites, cream of tartar and remaining vanilla until soft peaks form. Gradually add remaining sugar to eggs and beat at high speed until stiff peaks form. Plop on pie and work from center to edge to seal. Bake at 350° for 12-13 minutes or until meringue browns.

Chocolate Pies

HERSHEY BAR PIE

A popular 1970s era pie, the Hershey Bar Pie appears in more than 50 of the Arkansas cookbooks I have gathered.

1/2 pound Hershey bars, plain or almond, broken in half
1/2 cup milk
20 large marshmallows (approximately 1/2 bag)
1 - 8 ounce carton Cool Whip
1 teaspoon vanilla
1/4 teaspoon salt
1 baked 9 inch pastry pie crust or prepared chocolate cookie pie crust

Melt Hershey bars, milk and marshmallows together over low heat, stirring constantly. Cool completely. Fold vanilla and salt into Cool Whip, then fold into chocolate mix. Pour into prepared pie shell. Chill two hours before serving.

MOCKINGBIRD PIE

Chrissy Sanderson and Leigh Helms created Mockingbird Kitchen: Modern Ozark Dining to showcase the area's fine local produce, meats and food traditions. Their beautifully simple, Audubon bird themed restaurant in a peaceful strip mall corner showcases gorgeously lush interpretations of regional cuisine - and adds a fanciful touch on a dessert descended from the ever-popular Four Layer Delight.

Crust
4 ounces (1 stick) butter   4 ounces pecans
3 ounces all-purpose flour   Pinch salt

Preheat oven to 350°. Add flour and butter to food processor. Pulse until crumbly. Remove to separate bowl. Add pecans and salt to the food processor and pulse until the size of the flour and butter mix Stir all the ingredients together.

In an 8-inch pie pan press the dough mix down to form an even crust. Bake for 15 minutes or until crust starts to brown on the edges. Remove and refrigerate.

Cream cheese layer
4 ounces (1/2 block) cream cheese   1/2 cup confectioners' sugar
6 ounces heavy whipping cream

Beat cream cheese in electric mixer with paddle attachment until lumps are smooth. Add powdered sugar and cream and mix until smooth. Set aside.

Pastry cream layer
1/2 cup sugar   4 ounces chocolate
2 cups milk   2 ounces butter
1 teaspoon vanilla   2 ounces cornstarch
pinch Kosher salt   4 eggs

Heat sugar, milk, vanilla, and salt in a pot. Add the chocolate and butter In a separate bowl, mix cornstarch and eggs. Temper in the milk mixture into the egg mixture and return to a boil, stirring constantly, until it thickens like pudding. Strain and place in ice bath. Cover with plastic wrap so skin does not form. Set aside.

Whipped cream layer
2 cups heavy cream   6 ounces sugar

Beat together cream and sugar until tight (peaks form). Set aside.

Chocolate Pies

To assemble

Once crust has cooled, add cream cheese mixture and spread evenly. Place chocolate pastry cream in a plastic piping bag and pipe cream over cream cheese mixture. Smooth to even. Top with whipped cream layer and smooth crust.

Top with chopped pecans and cocoa nibs (optional). Cover and refrigerate overnight.

OREO PIE

This classic comes from the *Eureka Springs Chocolate Lovers' Festival Cookbook*, a tome of all sorts of chocolate delights. I've been fortunate to judge at the festival several times, and hope to again in the future. Tough work, but someone has to do it.

32 Oreo cookies
1/4 cup butter
2 cups milk
2 small packages instant chocolate pudding
1 - 8 ounce container whipped topping

Finely crush 24 of the cookies; mix with melted butter. Press firmly to bottom and sides of a 9-inch pie pan.

Pour milk into large bowl. Add pudding mixes. Beat with a wire whisk 2 minutes or until well blended and thick. Spoon a cup and a half of pudding into the crust. Gently stir half of the whipped topping into the remaining pudding; spread over pudding layer in the crust. Chop remaining cookies and stir into remaining whipped topping. Spread over pie. Chill for at least four hours before serving.

Chocolate Pies

POSSUM PIE

Myrtie Mae's Possum Pie is done in what is considered to be the default combination for home cooks - utilizing pudding mixes to reduce preparation times. The recipe comes from the Eureka Springs restaurant Myrtie Mae's, housed inside the Best Western Inn of the Ozarks. The restaurant is a descendant of the original operation by Myrtie Mae Bennett, who opened her living and dining rooms to travelers looking for a hot meal. She would reportedly welcome a guest, seat then, go kill and pluck a chicken in her backyard and have a complete fried chicken dinner on the table within an hour - fast food for the 1930s. And yes, huckleberry was the original pie offered.

1 prepared graham cracker crust
6 ounces cream cheese, softened
3/4 cup confectioners' sugar
1/4 cup chopped pecans
1/3 cup instant chocolate pudding mix
1/4 cup instant vanilla pudding mix
2 cups cold milk
3/4 teaspoon vanilla extract
1/2 cup heavy cream, whipped
12 to 16 pecan halves

In a mixing bowl, beat cream cheese and sugar until smooth. Spread onto bottom of crust. Sprinkle with chopped pecans.

In another mixing bowl, combine pudding mixes. Add milk and vanilla extract; beat on low speed for 2 minutes. Spoon over the pecans. Refrigerate for at least 2 hours. Top with whipped cream and pecan halves before serving.

TOLL HOUSE PIE

Renee Reynolds shares this cookie pie recipe in the *Arkansas Children's Hospital Cookbook* put out by the Little Rock Sam's Club - one of dozens of recipes I've found for this pie statewide over the years. I suspect it originated on the back of a chocolate chip package.

2 eggs
1/2 cup flour
1/2 cup sugar
1/2 cup firmly packed light brown sugar
3/4 cup butter, softened
1 cup chopped walnuts
6 ounces semi-sweet chocolate chips
1 unbaked 9 inch pastry pie shell
whipped cream or ice cream

Preheat oven to 325°. In large mixer bowl, beat eggs at high speed until foamy, about three minutes. Beat in flour, sugar and brown sugar until well-blended. Beat in softened butter. Stir in walnuts and chips. Pour into pie shell. Bake 55-60 minutes or until knife inserted halfway between edge and center comes out clean and top is golden brown. Cool on wire rack. Serve with whipped cream and ice cream, if desired.

MERINGUE PIES

BURNT SUGAR PIE

A good caramelized sugar pie has a flavor similar to the dulcet notes you get in a good crème brûlée. The caramel meringue pie from Charlotte's Eats and Sweets in Keo is a good example of the flavor to be sought in a pie like this. Though I have yet to be able to obtain that recipe, this one from *Arkansas Heritage: Recipes Past and Present*, published by the Arkansas Division of the American Cancer Society in 1992, does a good job of sharing that sort of flavor.

2 cups sugar
1/4 cup flour
2 egg yolks, beaten
2 cups milk
1 teaspoon vanilla extract

1 baked 9-inch pie shell
2 egg whites
3 Tablespoons confectioners' sugar

Brown 1/2 cup sugar in heavy saucepan over medium heat until amber colored, stirring constantly. Combine flour and remaining sugar in a bowl; mix well. Combine egg yolks, milk and vanilla in a bowl; mix well. Add to flour mixture; mix well. Stir into browned sugar. Cook until mixture is thickened, stirring constantly. Pour into baked pie shell. Beat egg whites until soft peaks form. Add confectioners' sugar gradually, beating until soft peaks form. Spread over top of pie, sealing to edge of pie. Bake at 350° for five minutes or until meringue is light brown.

Meringue Pies

CARAMEL PIE

From the moment she heard I was working on this book, my mom's been urging me to get this recipe in it from my aunt, Tommye Billing.

3 eggs, separated
1-1/2 cups sugar
5 Tablespoons flour
2 cups milk
1/8 teaspoon salt

2 Tablespoons butter
1 teaspoon vanilla
1/4 teaspoon cream of tartar
1 baked 9 inch pie crust

Beat egg yolks lightly. Add milk. Combine 1/4 cup sugar and the flour and add to the egg mixture. Add salt. Cook over medium heat until thick, stirring constantly. Remove from heat.

In an iron skillet or heavy saucepan, place one cup sugar and the butter. Stir and cook together until sugar is dissolved and reaches an amber color.

Pour custard into sugar mixture, stirring constantly until blended. Add vanilla. Pour into baked pie shell.

Heat oven to 350°. Beat egg whites until glossy and smooth. Add cream of tartar. Add 1/4 cup sugar a tablespoon at a time, beating in-between each addition, until stiff peaks form.

Pile meringue on pie, making sure to seal it to the edges and completely cover the filling. Bake about four inches away from heating element, until meringue is browned to desired color. Do not overbake.

GOOSEBERRY HANDMADE PIES CHOCOLATE ITALIAN MERINGUE PIE

Utilizing a lard crust (see page 26 for recipe), this rich pie is decadent and beautiful. Start by blind baking half a recipe of that crust, or whichever you'd like to use.

Filling
1-1/4 cups sugar
3 Tablespoons cornstarch
1/4 teaspoon salt
2 cups cold milk
2 ounces unsweetened chocolate
　(100% cacao)
3 eggs yolks
2 Tablespoons butter

Meringue
3 egg whites
1 cup sugar
1/2 cup water
1/4 teaspoon cream of tartar

1 baked 9 inch pastry pie crust

Whisk sugar, cornstarch and salt together. Add milk and chocolate and stir constantly over low heat, whisking together until chocolate is completely melted. If specks of chocolate remain after the mixture thickens, whisk rapidly.

Beat egg yolks and temper with a little of the chocolate mixture before pouring into the pot with other ingredients. Cook another two minutes, stirring constantly. Remove from heat, add butter and stir until butter is fully incorporated. Pour into blind baked pie crust and make meringue.

Place egg whites and cream of tartar in a stand mixer bowl. In a small saucepot, place the sugar and water over medium heat and cook until it reaches 240°. Turn stand mixer on high and whip whites to stiff peaks. Slowly drizzle the sugar water into the beaten egg whites and continue to whip another 1-2 minutes. Pile meringue on custard and bake until brown.

Meringue Pies

CHOCOLATE PIE WITH MERINGUE

This recipe with an unusual crust ingredient belongs to Sandra Halcumb.

Filling
1 cup sugar
3-1/2 Tablespoons cornstarch
3 Tablespoons cocoa
1/4 teaspoon salt
2 cups milk, divided
3 egg yolks
2 Tablespoons butter
1 teaspoon vanilla

Pie crust
1 cup flour
1/4 teaspoon salt
1/3 cup vegetable shortening
3 Tablespoons orange juice

Meringue
3 egg whites
1/4 teaspoon cream of tartar
1/2 teaspoon vanilla
1/3 cup sugar

Sift flour and salt together. Cut shortening into flour until it is crumb-like. Sprinkle 3 tablespoons orange juice over dough blend and mix until it holds together. Roll out onto floured surface or pat out into 9 inch pie plate. and bake at 375° until golden.

In a saucepan over medium heat, combine first four ingredients. Add 1/2 cup milk and whisk until smooth. Add yolks and blend well. Slowly add in remaining milk and cook until the custard thickens and begins to slightly bubble. Remove from heat and stir in butter and vanilla. Set aside.

Beat egg whites until stiff peaks form. Add rest of meringue ingredients. Beat until glossy.

Pour filling into crust, pile meringue on top, move to oven and brown lightly at 350° for about 12 minutes.

CHOCOLATE MERINGUE PIE

In Ruth Malone's 1961 book *Where To Eat in the Ozarks*, this recipe from the Buffalo River Dining Hall, a short distance down Arkansas Highway 14 from what was then Buffalo River State Park, appears alongside Winnie Todd's hush puppy recipe. Ten years later, the Buffalo would be named America's first National River.

1 baked 9 inch pastry pie shell	2 large egg yolks, beaten
3/4 cup sugar	1 Tablespoon butter
4 Tablespoons flour	1 teaspoon vanilla
1/4 teaspoon salt	
4 level Tablespoons cocoa	*Meringue:*
2 cups milk	2 large egg whites
	2 Tablespoons sugar

Mix sugar, flour, salt and cocoa. Add to milk and egg yolks and cook together until thick and creamy. Add butter and vanilla at the last. Pour into pie shell.

Beat egg whites until peaks form; add sugar and beat until peaks are stiff. Top pie with meringue and toast at 400° for 10 minutes. Cool before serving.

Benton's long-running Ed and Kay's Restaurant closed in 2014, the end of more than 60 years for the eatery on a bluff over the Saline River. The spot on the southwest side of town started out as Pat's Cafe, originally opened by Pat Newcomb. He built a little two room structure there and offered food from it, with no set hours. The place would do the standard meat-and-three and close when food ran out.

Pat hired Alma French in the 1960s to wait tables. Betwixt the two, the Mile High Meringue Pie was born. Alma and her husband Ed would eventually purchase the place in 1969 after Pat suffered a heart attack. The Frenches changed the name and kept going.

When they decided to retire, a different Ed entered the picture - Ed Diemer. He and his wife Kay took over in 1982, and painted the new name on the roof so it could be seen from the rather new stretch of Interstate 30 that passed right by the restaurant. Miss Alma stayed for a month after the Diemers bought the place and taught Kay - who stepped into that kitchen without knowing the ins and outs of restaurant cooking yet - everything the place served. Those Mile High Pies stayed on the menu, and over the course of the next several decades became regionally famous.

I was there the day Kay decided she was ready to be done. This time around, the recipes did not pass from one owner to the next. Though a couple different enterprises have occupied the spot since, the memories of those pies lingers.

My friend Cindy Martin Corbitt has shared with me recipes from *The Safety Zone Cookbook by Realtors and Other Famous People* from 1995, contributed by original pie maker Alma French.

MISS ALMA'S CHOCOLATE MERINGUE PIE

A perennial favorite from the restaurant. Like all of Miss Alma's meringues, this includes about a half cup of crushed ice, which leaves the meringue moist and with tiny air pockets.

Custard
2 cups milk
1 Tablespoon salted butter
2 heaping Tablespoons cornstarch
2 heaping Tablespoons cocoa powder
pinch of salt
water
4 or 5 egg yolks
1 teaspoon vanilla
2/3 cups sugar

Meringue
1 cup egg whites (6-8)
pinch of salt
crushed ice
1 heaping Tablespoon cornstarch
1/4 teaspoon cream of tartar
1/3 cup sugar
1/4 teaspoon vanilla

1 baked 9 inch pastry pie crust

Heat the milk with butter. Mix dry ingredients together. Add enough water to moisten. Add egg yolks to this; mix well. Add to boiling milk; stir well until thick. Add vanilla. Pour into baked pie shell and allow to cool.

Put egg whites in mixer bowl. Add crushed ice; beat on high until fluffy. Add remaining ingredients and beat until thick and full. Pile on top of cooled pie. Brown in oven at 300°. Cool completely before serving.

MAUDE BRANNON'S COCONUT PIE

My friend Tom Brannon is known for many things, particularly as the chief meteorologist at THV 11 here in Little Rock and as an extraordinary supporter and fundraiser for the Arkansas Foodbank. His parents operated one of Cabot's most beloved restaurants. His grandmother Maude, though, is the person who created this marvelous recipe for coconut pie.

2 cups milk
1 cup + 1 Tablespoon sugar
2 heaping Tablespoons cornstarch
3/4 cup coconut (plus extra for garnish)
3 eggs
2 Tablespoons butter
1 teaspoon vanilla
1 baked 9 inch pastry pie crust

Heat oven to 350°. Separate the eggs, whites in a bowl and yellows in a cup. Combine the first three ingredients in a saucepan over medium heat. Stir the mix until it comes to a boil.

Take the yellows and some mixture in the cup to combine them (temper the eggs with a little mix and then return to the saucepan). Keep stirring until you have mixed the ingredients. Place the butter and vanilla into the saucepan, keep stirring. The last thing is the coconut into the pan, stir it roughly into the mix. Pour the mixture into the pie crust.

Beat the egg whites until foamy, then add one tablespoon sugar and beat until peaks form. Place on top of pie. Sprinkle with coconut. Brown in 350° oven.

Meringue Pies

COCONUT CREAM MERINGUE PIE

One of the most distant restaurants you'll find across Arkansas is the cafe within the Oark General Store. There's no cell reception, though there is free wifi if you need to send a message. Breakfasts are country-style, burgers are thick, and the onion rings are righteous. And if the coconut meringue pie is in the case, it's worth a slice. This is Miss Cathie's recipe, and it makes two pies.

1/4 cup cornstarch	8 egg yolks
1 1/3 cup sugar	4 Tablespoons butter, softened
6 cups milk OR	2 teaspoons vanilla
1 can evaporated milk	2 cups coconut
plus 2 cups fresh milk	2 baked 9 inch pastry pie crusts

Mix together and cook cornstarch, sugar, milks, and egg yolks over medium heat, stirring constantly, until mixture begins to bubble. Count to 30 while continuing to stir. Remove from heat and add coconut, vanilla and butter. Pour into two pie crusts.

12 egg whites	4 Tablespoons sugar
1 Tablespoon cream of tartar	1/2 cup coconut

Beat egg whites and cream of tartar together until soft peaks form. Add sugar and beat until peaks are firm.

Add meringue to top of pie, starting in center and spreading outward. Be sure to seal meringue to edge of pie shell. Sprinkle with remaining coconut and bake at 350° for 15 minutes or until meringue browns.

COCONUT MERINGUE PIE

My aunt Beverly Sanders uses this recipe not just for her coconut meringue pie, but sometimes leaves out the coconut and uses the filling recipe for banana pudding, too.

Filling
1 cup sugar
1/4 cup flour
2 egg yolks
1-1/3 cups milk
1 small can evaporated milk
1 cup sweetened coconut
1 teaspoon vanilla
pinch of salt
1/4 cup butter
1 unbaked 9 inch pie crust

Meringue
2 to 4 egg whites
2 Tablespoons sugar for every egg white
1/8 teaspoon cream of tartar for each egg white

Preheat oven to 350°.

In a large saucepan mix sugar, flour, salt, egg yolks and milk. Cook until thick on medium heat, stirring to prevent sticking and lumping. When thick, turn off heat. Add vanilla, margarine and coconut and stir. Stir until butter is melted.

Pour in baked pie crust and add meringue. Bake until meringue is done. Slightly browned peaks. Watch closely. Cool. Serve hot or refrigerate in a pie container in the refrigerator when completely cool.

For meringue: Beat egg whites on high speed with an electric mixer until it reaches stiff peaks. Add sugar and cream of tartar. Beat with mixer on high until stiff peaks.

Spread over pie being sure the meringue touches the crust. With spatula, tap the pie gently and raise to get peaks.

Bake pie in 350° oven. Watch closely. Cook until peaks are light brown.

Meringue Pies

COCONUT CREAM PIE

Another great recipe from The Purple Cow, that showcases the sort of pie every diner should have in its pie case.

1 unbaked 9 inch pastry pie crust

Filling
3/4 cup sugar
1/3 cup flour
1/4 teaspoon salt
2 cups milk
3 egg yolks
2 Tablespoons butter
1 teaspoon vanilla
1 cup sweetened coconut flakes

Meringue
4 egg whites
1/2 cup sugar
2/3 teaspoon cream of tartar
1/4 cup coconut

Heat oven to 450°. Prick pie crust all over with a fork. Bake for 13-15 minutes, until golden brown. Allow to cool.

Separate the egg yolks from whites, making sure absolutely no yolk gets into the whites. Leave the whites to sit at room temperature. Beat yolks.

Mix sugar, flour and salt thoroughly in a bowl. Stir in the milk and dissolve dry ingredients completely. Cook over medium high heat, stirring constantly, until custard thickens and comes to a boil. Do not scorch. Slow boil two minutes, continuing to stir. Remove from heat.

Stir a small portion of the hot liquid into the yolks, then return to the saucepan the warmed yolk mixture and continue to boil two more minutes while stirring. Remove from heat, add butter, vanilla and coconut, and stir to incorporate. Pour into pie shell and allow to cool 15 minutes before topping with meringue.

Beat the egg whites until they reach 7x their unbeaten volume. Add the cream of tartar and continue to beat another 30 seconds. Gradually add the sugar..Lay the meringue onto the pie and spread to edges to seal. Brown in 350°oven for 12-15 minutes. Serve at room temperature, or refrigerate if not serving immediately.

LEMON CREAM MERINGUE PIE

This recipe combines the flavor of a lemon cream pie with the meringue of... well, a meringue pie. It's bright, sweet, tart, and a real hit - my favorite meringue pie to make, from a recipe from Claudia Ellis of Glenville Elementary.

Filling
2 cans Eagle Brand sweetened condensed milk
3 egg yolks
juice of 3 lemons
1 small package vanilla wafers *or* 1 prepared 9 inch graham cracker crust

Meringue
1 Tablespoon lemon juice
3 Tablespoons cornstarch
6 Tablespoons sugar
3 egg whites

Heat oven to 325°. Mix Eagle Brand milk, yolks and lemon juice for filling together. Pour into pie crust. Bake for 20-25 minutes. Remove from oven and increase heat to 350°.

Beat egg whites until soft peaks form. Beat in remaining ingredients until peaks are stiff. Lay into center of pie and work out towards edges. Place back in oven for 10 minutes to brown. Allow to cool, then refrigerate until time to serve.

Meringue Pies

LEMON MERINGUE PIE

Another one of the great Mile High Pies Miss Alma French made for Ed and Alma's restaurant. Use the meringue recipe from the chocolate meringue pie recipe on page 199.

1-3/4 cups water
1-1/3 cups sugar
3 heaping Tablespoons cornstarch
salt
1/2 cup lemon juice
4 to 5 egg yolks
1 baked 9 inch pie shell

Heat the water. Mix the sugar, starch, salt and just enough lemon juice to moisten the dry ingredients. Add the remaining lemon juice to the water. Beat 4-5 yolks and add to dry ingredients. Add all to lemon water and cook until thick and clear. Pour into pie shell. Top with meringue and brown.

LEMON MERINGUE PIE

Nobia Lee Jeffrey Bufford contributed this recipe to *Cooking Kin: The Favorite Recipes of the Jeffrey-Alexander Cousins* from 1986.

1 baked 9 inch pastry pie shell
4 eggs, separated
1/3 cup cornstarch
2 cups sugar, divided into 1-1/2 cups and 1/2 cup measures
1/4 teaspoon salt
1-1/2 cups water
2 Tablespoons grated lemon peel
2 Tablespoons butter
1/2 cup lemon juice
1/4 teaspoon cream of tartar

Separate eggs, and beat egg yolks slightly. In a small saucepan, combine cornstarch, one and a half cups sugar, and salt. Gradually add water, stirring until smooth. Over medium heat, bring to boil for 1 minute, stirring occasionally. Remove from heat. Stir in lemon juice, lemon peel, and butter. Pour into pie shell.

Preheat oven to 400°. Beat egg whites with cream of tartar at medium speed until soft peaks form. Gradually beat in remaining sugar two tablespoonfuls at a time. Continue until stiff peaks form. Spread over filling. Bake 7 to 9 minutes or until brown.

Meringue Pies

LEMON MERINGUE PIE

This version of the classic comes from Miss Mary's, a sweet breakfast and lunch joint near the heart of Gentry, where you can absolutely have pie for breakfast and no one will judge you. Miss Mary's has a large number of pies rotating through the line-up. This lemon meringue pie is quite popular.

Filling

1-1/2 cups sugar
1/3 cup + 1 Tablespoon cornstarch
1 1/2 cups water
3 egg yolks, slightly beaten
3 Tablespoons butter
2 teaspoons lemon zest
1/2 cup lemon juice
1 baked pastry pie crust

Heat oven to 400°. Mix sugar and cornstarch in 2 quart saucepan. Stir in water gradually. Cook over medium heat, stirring constantly, until thickened. Boil one minute.

Temper egg yolks with about half of hot mixture. Boil and stir one minute more. Remove from heat.

Whisk in butter and lemon zest. Whisk in lemon juice and pour into pie shell.

Meringue

3 egg whites at room temperature
1/4 teaspoon cream of tartar
6 Tablespoons sugar
1/2 teaspoon vanilla

Cover hot mixture with meringue. Spread to edges of crust and seal.

Bake until delicate brown (about 10 minutes). Cool away from draft at room temperature.

ORANGE MERINGUE PIE

Mrs. Gary Goldman is credited with this 1970 recipe in the St. Paul United Methodist Church *85th Anniversary Cookbook*, published in 1995.

1 cup sugar, divided
1/4 cup cornstarch
1/4 teaspoon salt
1-1/2 cup orange juice
2 slightly beaten egg yolks

1 Tablespoon butter
1 teaspoon grated orange peel
8 or 9 inch baked pastry shell
2 egg whites

In saucepan combine 3/4 cup sugar, cornstarch and salt. Gradually stir in orange juice. Cook and stir over high heat til thickened and bubbly. Reduce heat; cook 1 minute more; remove from heat. Temper egg yolks with small amount of orange liquid, then incorporate into mixture. Cook and stir over medium heat for another two minutes. Stir in butter and orange peel. Pour into pastry shell.

Beat egg whites to soft peaks; gradually beat in remaining sugar til stiff peaks form. Spread meringue over hot filling, sealing to edge of crust. Bake at 400° for 7-9 minutes. Cool several hours before serving.

PEANUT BUTTER MERINGUE PIE

Lisa Hackett ran the famed Mona Lisa Cafe in Shirley for many years. This is one of her favorites.

1 baked pastry pie shell
1/2 cup peanut butter
1/2 cup sugar
2 cups milk
2 Tablespoons butter
1 cup confectioners sugar
1/4 cup cornstarch
1/4 teaspoon salt
3 eggs, separated
1/2 teaspoon vanilla

Mix powdered sugar and peanut butter together until it feels like cornmeal. Mix cornstarch, sugar, salt and egg yolks together; add milk, butter and vanilla. Cook over low heat until thickened. Put powdered sugar and peanut butter mixture into pie mixture and stir just a little.

Pour into baked pie shell. Top with beaten egg whites. Bake at 325° until light brown, about 15 minutes.

RHUBARB CREAM PIE

The standard flavors for meringue pies tend to be coconut, chocolate, and lemon with a small smattering of other choices. So when I came across this recipe in the 1976 *Favorite Recipes* cookbook by the Bismarck Council of the Telephone Pioneers of America, I was intrigued. Dorothy Pfau of Dickinson shared this unusual combination. I did find it a bit syrupy, but tasty.

3 cups sliced rhubarb
1 cup sugar
3 Tablespoons flour
3 egg yolks
3 Tablespoons sour cream
1/2 teaspoon cinnamon
1 Tablespoon cold butter, sliced
1 unbaked 9 inch pastry pie crust
3 egg whites
1/4 teaspoon cream of tartar
1/2 cup sugar

Heat oven to 400°. Beat together sugar and eggs. Add in flour and sour cream. Fold in rhubarb. Pour into pie shell. Sprinkle cinnamon and place slices of butter over the top of filling. Shield pie edges. Bake for 10 minutes, then reduce heat to 350° and bake another 40 minutes. Allow to cool completely.

Beat egg whites until soft peaks form. Add cream of tartar and sugar and continue to beat until meringue is shiny. Spread over pie. Bake at 350° until meringue is golden.

HUCKLEBERRY PIE

Huckleberry pie is a classic dish from all through Arkansas that has gone into decline – mostly because it's hard to get wild-picked huckleberries these days. The sole location where you can still find huckleberry pie on the menu is at the Balcony Restaurant atop the Basin Park Hotel in downtown Eureka Springs. Here, it's a fried pie, filled with huckleberries, served with huckleberry ice cream.

5 cups wild blue huckleberries
1-1/2 cups sugar
6 Tablespoons cornstarch
4 Tablespoons flour
1 teaspoon grated lemon rind (fresh)
Prepared biscuit mix
   or packaged biscuit dough

Mix the above ingredients together with a spoon so that everything is well distributed

Roll biscuit dough to 1/4 inch height. Cut into 6 inch circles. Spoon 3 ounces into middle of circle. Moisten one half of edge with water and fold in half. Crimp edges using the tines of a fork and freeze on a flat service lined with parchment paper.

To coo,k put about 3 inches of oil in a cast iron skillet. Heat to 350° degrees. Carefully place pie in hot oil for 8 minutes each side. Use a slotted spoon or tongs to remove pie onto a paper towel to drain. Serve garnished with powdered sugar.

LITTLE FRIED PIES

An interesting musing on fried pies appears in *Our Family Favorites: Edmondson Family Cookbook*, published in 1986. This isn't so much a full recipe as a rumination on how to make them. I will say, it's the only recipe I've collected from our state that includes jelly as its main filling ingredient, outside of the random PB&J pies I've encountered.

Roll out pie crust or biscuits about the size of a saucer. Sprinkle half the dough with mixture of cinnamon and sugar (equal parts) and a good size pat of butter. Fold over, crimp, and fry. Drain and sprinkle with sugar. Sometimes Mama would make us these and use only a spoonful of jelly inside.

FRIED PIE SECRETS

When I started to compile this book, I thought I'd have a lot more recipes for fried pes. Turns out, that's not the case, for a very simple reason - fried pies are, for the most part, a quick and easy food created from what's on hand. The filling is usually whatever you have left over, whether it's something sweet or savory. I've personally made fried pies filled with Swedish meatballs, turkey and dressing, and even tuna casserole, as well as fresh fruit, chocolate, whole caramels, and thick pudding.

A fried pie's crust can be a traditional pie crust, fillo dough, biscuit mix, pre-packaged biscuits, wonton wrappers, and doughnut dough. The pastry itself is not as important as what it contains - because you're essentially creating a pocket to carry your food in. Much like the coffyns of medieval times, where a filling was baked in a crust and the crust wasn't eaten, the crust is a conveyance.

Best of all, a fried pie doesn't even need to be fried in this day and age. While the term hand pie is more appropriate, the fried pie name has just stuck, even when the individual pie is oven baked. So enjoy any recipe within as a filling for a fried pie.

OLD FASHIONED CHOCOLATE FRIED PIES

I recall this pie from childhood. My paternal grandmother would sometimes make these in the skillet that was always on the stove with about an inch of Crisco or bacon fat in it. The simple filling of flour, confectioners' sugar and butter, all easy things to keep and acquire, always brings me back to being a young girl and enjoying the treat. Today, you can get a marvelous version at Batten's Bakery in Paragould. There are also fried pies like this at Snappy Food Marts in Bee Branch and Damascus. Or you can make them yourself at home.

1/2 cup sugar
1/4 cup flour
1 Tablespoon unsweetened
    cocoa powder
1 cup milk

2 Tablespoons butter
1/2 teaspoon vanilla
2 cups biscuit mix
cooking oil (for frying)
confectioners' sugar (for dusting)

In a saucepan combine sugar, flour, and unsweetened cocoa powder. Stir in 1/2 cup milk and butter. Cook over medium heat until the mixture is thickened and bubbly, stirring constantly. Stir in vanilla. Allow to cool.

In a mixing bowl stir together the biscuit mix and 1/2 cup milk. On a well-floured surface, knead the dough 12 times. Roll the dough to 1/8 inch thickness. Cut dough into twelve inch circles.

Place one tablespoon filling in the center of each circle of dough circle. Brush the edge of the dough with water. Fold the dough over the filling; press the edges together with tines of a fork to seal.

In a skillet heat one inch cooking oil to 375° degrees. Fry the pastries for about two minutes, or until golden. Turn once. Drain on paper towel and sprinkle warm pastries with sifted cconfectioners' sugar.

OLD FASHIONED CHOCOLATE HAND PIES

Want to bake your pies instead? Use the recipe right before this, or this one right here. Or fry the pies in this recipe. They're interchangeable!

2 cups sugar
1/2 cup cocoa powder

1/2 cup (one stick) butter
2 prepared pie crust crusts

Heat oven to 350° degrees. In a skillet or saucepot, combine sugar, cocoa powder and butter over low heat until incorporated into a paste. Roll out pie dough thin. Use a biscuit cutter or a tuna can cleaned with the bottom cut out to cut hand pie doughs. Place a tablespoon of filling in each one. Crimp the edges with a fork. Place on a baking sheet and bake 20 minutes or until dough is golden. Serve hot with ice cold milk, or save for later.

OZARK FOLK CENTER FRIED PIES

During the summer months, one of the on-park restaurants at the Ozark Folk Center sometimes offers these golden beauties for snacking while enjoying the craft village. It's a good, solid recipe for a great fried pie crust.

3 ounces evaporated milk
1/2 cup water
1/2 cup shortening (stick of Crisco), melted
1 ounce white vinegar
2 cups self-rising flour
1/2 cup plain flour
Filling (chocolate custard, cooked fruit mélange, etc.)

Mix together evaporated milk, water, shortening and white vinegar. Blend flour into liquid. Using an electric mixer, mix until texture of dough is silky, not sticky or dry. Adjust with small amounts of liquid if too dry to roll or small amount of flour if sticky.

Pull an amount the size of a big walnut and roll into ball. Roll into a six-inch circle on floured board or parchment paper.

Place a tablespoon of any type of filling toward one side of the circle. Brush the edges of the circle with evaporated milk. Fold in half and seal edges with fork or fingers. Punch holes in the top using a fork two times. This prevents explosion.

Use vegetable oil to deep fry at temperature of 350° degrees for 5 minutes or until golden brown. If you pan fry, turn pies when first side browns.

Fried Pies and Hand Pies

SWEET POTATO HAND PIES

This is one of the recipes I developed during my time writing *A Bite of Arkansas*, when pandemic downtime allowed me the hours to experiment with different ideas and cook to my heart's content. This is a nice, clean flavored recipe. I would suggest adding an egg wash for crust color.

1.5 pounds sweet potato
2 Tablespoons real maple syrup
1/2 teaspoon vanilla
1/2 teaspoon cinnamon
1/4 teaspoon salt
2 unbaked 9 inch pastry pie crusts

Boil or bake sweet potatoes. Remove skin. Mash (don't purée) together with syrup, vanilla, cinnamon and salt.

Roll both pie dough balls flat into circles. Cut in half. Arrange a quarter of the filling on one side with one inch dough left around side. Fold over and crimp with a fork. Bake at 350° for 35-40 minutes. Serve hot or cold.

The Great Arkansas Pie Book

```
                        FRIED PIES

Biscuit dough                       Sugar
Peaches                             Bacon grease

Roll out biscuit dough size of salad plate.  Cook dried peaches
real soft so they can be mashed, add sugar to taste.  Have hot
bacon grease ready to fry pies.  Drain on paper towels.

Myra Nisler was a member of our church and had quite a lot to do
with the Cumberland Presbyterian Church, especially working with
the children.
                                    Submitted by Judy Calhoun
                                71
```

PIES
that make their own crust

LASHLEE STEEL COMPAN[Y]

STEEL FABRICATORS  BUILDING SPECIALTIES

> This crustless custard pie recipe was found handwritten on a piece of paper stuck in a cookbook owned by Mrs. M.W. Koehler, dated 1967 and either gifted or purchased at the Hotel Marion.

Custard Pie

Blend 1½ cup sugar
⅓ cup flour — blender
heat 2 cups milk with
½ stick Oleo add to sugar
+ flour and blend
add 4 eggs 1 tea vinella
blend 6 min. pour into
9 in pan (buttered)
sprinkle with nutmeg.
and bake at 325° about
25 min

MATERIAL CAN BE BOUGHT MANY PLACES — WE SELL S[TEEL]

Pies That Make Their Own Crust

FUDGE BROWNIE PIE

It's almost brownies, easy to make, travels well, and to my partner (who ate three of six of these pies I made during research) absolutely irresistible. This makes-its-own-crust pie is a recipe to memorize. This version comes from Johnna Morley of the River Valley Squares, and was printed in the Arkansas State Square Dance Federation's 1990 cookbook.

1 cup sugar
1 stick melted butter
2 eggs
1/2 cup flour
dash salt
5 Tablespoons cocoa
1 teaspoon vanilla
1/2 cup chopped nuts of choice (optional)

Beat sugar and butter until creamy. Add remaining ingredients. Beat well. Add nuts. Pour in pie plate. Bake at 300° for 30 minutes. Top with vanilla ice cream or beaten heavy cream. Serve warm or cold.

GOODY PIE

Mrs. B.W. Jackson submitted this recipe for the 1980 *In Good Taste* cookbook put out by the El Dorado Service League. It is quite similar to the Osgood pie, with the exception here being pineapple instead of raisins. Both pies, being relatives of the chess pie, take their name from "it's a good pie."

3 egg whites
1-1/2 cup sugar
2 Tablespoons Karo syrup
1 lemon rind, grated
Juice of 1/2 lemon
22 Ritz crackers, crushed
1 cup pineapple tidbits, drained
1 cup pecans, chopped
Butter to grease pie plate
1 cup heavy cream
1/2 teaspoon lemon extract
2 teaspoons sugar for cream

Beat egg whites with sugar until stiff. Add Karo syrup and beat well. Add lemon rind and lemon juice. Mix crackers, pineapple, and pecans. Add to egg mixture. Turn out into buttered 9 inch pie plate. Bake at 300° for 1 hour. Add lemon extract and sugar to cream and beat until stiff. When pie cools, top with flavored cream.

This pie is better 2-3 days later. Refrigerate covered.

MAKES ITS OWN CRUST RAISIN PIE

Another Arkansas Sesquicentennial cookbook, *Pebbles Recipe Harvest*, contains several crustless pies - including this one that's like a big, soft cookie. It comes from Diana McWilliams.

1/4 cup butter
3/4 cup sugar
3 eggs
1 teaspoon vanilla
1-1/2 cups seedless raisins
1/2 cup chopped walnuts
1/2 of a 9.25 ounce pie crust mix
Whipped cream

Cream together butter and sugar. Add eggs and continue beating until light and fluffy. Add vanilla, raisins and walnuts. Crumble pie crust mix and add to mixture; stir well and spoon into a well-oiled 9 inch pie pan. Bake at 325° until pie is firm in center. Cool. Serve with whipped cream.

The Great Arkansas Pie Book

PARADISE PIE

When searching for any great Arkansas recipe, there are a few good standbys - *Little Rock Cooks* by the Junior League of Little Rock, *Sampling Arkansas* from the Arkansas Division of the American Cancer Society, and this book - *Feasts of Eden*. The cookbook was written by Ruby C. Thomas in 1990, showcasing the delights served at her restaurant at The Red Apple Inn. Ruby and her husband Herbert opened a lodge on Eden Isle in 1963. It burned down the next year, but in 1965 the new lodge and restaurant were constructed, and ever since, it's been an incredible destination. I go further into the history of Eden Isle and Greers Ferry Lake in my fourth book, *Another Slice of Arkansas Pie: A Guide to the Best Restaurants, Bakeries, Truck Stops and Food Trucks for Delectable Bites in The Natural State*.

Ruby Thomas put together *Feasts of Eden* from the standards she served at the restaurant over its decades. It showcases some of the finest cuisine offered in mid-century Arkansas - trout Almandine, spring lamb with baked stuffed onions, black eyed peas with green tomato pickle, mushroom eggplant casserole, all amazing dishes that combined Arkansas food with continental flair. Indeed, the images from her book, taken by Thomas S. Gordon, are some of the few that exist of our cuisine from that period of time - which did indeed inspire me to photograph the dishes included in *Arkansas Cookery*, to capture what they look like, not just the recipes.

Amongst the high-end, five star restaurant expectations from this haute cuisine, you'll find a recipe for the much-beloved Paradise Pie, which in itself is a humble, subsistance dessert. That's because this decadent pie is actually made from crackers!

3 egg whites
1 cup sugar
20 soda crackers
1 cup pecans, chopped
1 cup heavy cream, whipped
1 teaspoon vanilla
7 ounces grated coconut

Beat egg whites until almost stiff. Add sugar gradually while continuing to beat. Fold in crumbled crackers and nuts. Scrape into 9 inch pie plate that has been well buttered. Bake 20 minutes at 325°. Cool.

Beat heavy cream together with vanilla until glossy peaks form. Fold in coconut and spread across top of pie. Serve or refrigerate.

RICE PIE

There's more rice grown in Arkansas than in all 49 other United States, combined. That may sound crazy, but it's true - the Arkansas Delta and sections of the Arkansas River Valley are home to hundreds of rice farms. So it's no surprise that rice pie has been a thing for at least a century.

This is Bertha Evans' recipe as featured in *The Art of Cooking in Heber Springs*. I have found really nice success with this pie by substituting Ralston Farms rice grits - these are cut rice grains that are an excellent, silky smooth alternative to traditional corn grits.

4 eggs, beaten
1 teaspoon vanilla
2 cups milk
1/2 cup Bisquick
1/2 cup sugar
1/2 cup cooked rice
1/4 teaspoon salt

Beat eggs and vanilla together for two minutes. Add dry ingredients and beat two minutes. Pour into buttered pie pan. Bake in a 375° oven for 35 minutes. If not done, bake 10 minutes longer.

Pies That Make Their Own Crust

RITZ PIE

Kay McCall submitted this for the 1986 publication of *Pebbles Recipe Harvest*. The pie itself comes out with an almost brownie-crisp top with a lovely bite; if you don't add the whipped cream, be sure to serve this one with ice cold milk.

20 Ritz crackers
1 cup chopped pecans
1 cup sugar
1/2 pint whipping cream
3 egg whites
1 teaspoon vanilla

Crush crackers; add vanilla and pecans. Beat egg whites to soft peaks. Add sugar and continue to beat until peaks begin to shine and get stiff. Fold into cracker mixture.

Oil a 9 inch pie plate and pour in mixture. Bake 25-35 minutes at 325°. Let pie cool. Top with whipped cream, if desired. If so, let stand at least four hours in the refrigerator before serving.

The Great Arkansas Pie Book

SQUASH PIE

This pie appears in Tatum and Packer's *The Ozarks Collection*, published in 1987. For this testing, I tried using several different sorts of squash. I found that yellow squash and butternut squash were both really good contenders for use in this recipe - so, since I was testing in the heart of winter, I went for the latter for this photograph.

2 Tablespoons butter
1 quart squash, boiled, mashed and drained
1/2 cup sugar
2 eggs, well beaten
1/2 cup flour
1 teaspoon vanilla
2 teaspoons baking powder

Heat oven to 350°. Melt butter in warm, drained squash. Let cool. Combine sugar and beaten eggs. Add squash, flour, vanilla and baking powder. Turn into greased pie pan and bake for 40-50 minutes.

SAVORY PIES

18th CENTURY MEAT PIE

Many of the early dishes of the Ozarks come from English settlers who came here in the early 18th Century. British food has a long history with savory pies, documented back to the 12th century with coffyns, or pastry crusts made mostly of flour, salt, water and fat to create a cooking vessel for a filling. These outer shells were not always eaten - when they were, the top crust would be savored, while the bottom crust would be given to beggars at the gate. This is where we get the term "upper crust."

Billy Joe Tatum and Ann Taylor Packer examine much of what shaped our cuisine in their 1987 book *The Ozark Collection: The Best Recipes from the Heritage and Traditions of a Storied Region*. Their deep dive into food traditions of the Arkansas and Missouri Ozarks includes several recipes on what to do with leftovers. Pies were, in so many cases, the answer, featuring everything from bacon scraps to lamb kidneys.

This recipe is derived from their Meat Pie with Flaky Crust; while the book does give modern recipes later on for basic pastry, this version augments that by using beef fat cut from brisket as its pastry fat. It is pliant and quite good.

Crust

12 ounces all-purpose flour (about 2.25 cups)
1 cup beef fat cut from smoked or cooked brisket (any solid beef fat will do), diced and chilled
Up to 2 tablespoons salt (if meat is smoked and salted already, omit)
Up to 1/2 cup ice cold water

In food processor, place two thirds of flour and the salt (if using) and pulse five times. Place beef fat over surface of flour in processor. Pulse 20-25 times or until flour mix appears like crumbs. Pour in remaining flour and pulse five more times.

Turn dough into bowl and sprinkle with 2 tablespoons water. Press dough until it comes together. Separate into two balls. In separate ziptop bags, place one ball each and press into a four to five inch disk. Chill for one hour.

Savory Pies

Filling

2 cups cooked and chopped beef steak, brisket or well-drained ground beef
2/3 cups beef broth
1 beef bouillon cube (optional)
1/3 cup heavy cream or sour cream
1/2 teaspoon celery salt
1/4 teaspoon onion salt
1 rounded teaspoon flour
Pastry crust as listed on previous page
Butter or egg wash

Combine broth, seasonings and cream in medium saucepan, heating gradually.. When broth mix is hot, pour in flour and stir on and off until thickened. Add beef and coat all meat surfaces. Remove from heat.

Heat oven to 350°. Roll out one of the discs and fit to a 9-inch pie pan, making sure crust reaches just past outside edge. Fill with meat mixture. Roll out the other crust and place on top. Cut to pan size and roll top edge of crust under bottom edge all the way around. Brush entire top crust with butter or egg wash. Vent crust.

Bake 30-35 minutes or until top crust reaches desired golden brown-ness. Let rest 15 minutes before cutting. Once cooled, whole pie can be removed from pan, wrapped tightly in plastic, and frozen for up to one month.

The Great Arkansas Pie Book

BEEF PIE

This is a favorite pie Grav Weldon makes during the colder months.

2 unbaked 9 inch pastry crusts
2 pounds chuck roast, trimmed
Salt and pepper to taste
2 onions, chopped fine
1 Tablespoon Worcestershire
1 twelve ounce bag mixed vegetables
1 Tablespoon flour
1/2 cup water
Other seasonings as desired

Salt and pepper roast. Place roast, onions and Worcestershire sauce in Crock Pot on high heat for one hour. Reduce to medium heat and cook until beef shreds with a fork. Add vegetables. Make a slurry with flour and water and add. Cook over low heat one hour. Taste and season as desired. Let cool.

Line deep dish pie pan with one crust. Spoon beef mixture into crust. Cover with top crust, crimp and vent. Bake at 350° for 50-55 minutes. Rest pie for 10 minutes before cutting and serving.

Savory Pies

BRADLEY COUNTY PINK TOMATO PIE

Each year, thousands flock to the town of Warren for the annual Bradley County Pink Tomato Festival. The event celebrates the city's history as a hub of tomato production. There were once more than 80 tomato producers within the county lines. Today, there are seven. That doesn't keep anyone from celebrating the state's official fruit and vegetable with a carnival, concerts, a steak cook-off, pageants, and the All-Tomato Feast, which includes tomatoes in every dish, including dessert!

This pie is a savory pie, tangy, bright and substantial enough for a meal. Angela Norton originally contributed for *Another Slice of Arkansas Pie*. I suggest fresh garlic, basil and oregano for seasoning.

1 deep dish 9 inch pastry pie crust
3-5 large tomatoes, peeled, seeded and sliced to about 1/2" thick
1/2 teaspoon spices of choice (basil, parsley, garlic, oregano etc.)
1/2 teaspoon salt
1/2 teaspoon pepper
1 cup mayonnaise
3/4 cup grated cheddar cheese
3/4 cup grated mozzarella cheese
1/4 cup scallions or chives
6 strips cooked bacon (optional)

Bake pie shell for 10 minutes at 375°. Layer tomatoes in shell and sprinkle with salt, pepper, and additional herbs & spices if wanted. Mix together mayonnaise, cheeses and scallions or chives. Spread mixture over tomatoes in pie shell. Bake at 350° for 30 minutes until brown and bubbly. Crumble bacon on top. Allow to stand 5 minutes before serving.

BRISKET PIE

Expounding on the 18th Century Meat Pie recipe, I took an Arkansas favorite smoked meat - brisket - and made it into this pie. Start with the 18th century beef fat pie crust on page 231 or the Gooseberry Handmade Pies lard crust on page 26.

Top and bottom beef fat crusts
2 cups smoked and pulled beef brisket
1-1/2 teaspoon beef fat from brisket, finely chopped
1/2 cup chopped onion
1 cup reserve broth from drippings, or 1 cup beef broth
1 rounded teaspoon flour
1-1/2 teaspoons barbecue rub of choice
Butter or egg wash (optional)

Heat beef fat from brisket in skillet. Add onion and saute. Skim out onion and set aside. Make a roux with the flour, until the mixture just begins to thicken. Add broth and stir until well-dissolved.

Drop shredded beef into broth. Once all beef strands are coated, stir in your rub or seasoning. Cook until beef is warm throughout but not hot.

Heat oven to 350°. Lay bottom crust into pan. Fill with meat. Top with other crust and brush entire top with butter or egg wash. Vent. Bake 30-35 minutes or until top crust reaches desired brownness. Let rest 15 minutes before slicing. Serve with barbecue sauce.

Savory Pies

CHEESEBURGER PIE

Want pie for dinner? This quick make pie is excellent for a family meal you can make in advance. It works with a pastry crust but is even better in a biscuit crust. It comes from *Alpena Cooks* and was submitted by Lucretia Mills.

1 pound ground beef
1/2 cup evaporated milk
1/2 cup ketchup
1/3 cup breadcrumbs
1/4 cup chopped onion
1/2 teaspoon oregano
3/4 teaspoon salt
1/8 teaspoon pepper
1 unbaked pie crust of choice
4 ounces shredded Cheddar
1 teaspoon Worcestershire sauce

Combine first eight ingredients. Prepare pie crust, then fill with meat mixture. Toss cheese with Worcestershire sauce and spread across top of pie. Bake at 350° for 35-40 minutes. Let stand 10 minutes before serving.

The Great Arkansas Pie Book

CHICKEN PIE

I decided when I tackled this project that I was going to include savory pies in this book, because they're a big part of home cooking throughout our statehood and before. One of my goals was to come up with a perfect chicken pot pie that would represent our state well. So I started digging through historic recipes.

This particular version comes from *Thirty Years at the Mansion by Liza Ashley, as told to Carolyn Huber*. The book is an extraordinary collection of stories and recipes during eight Arkansas gubernatorial administrations by seven governors (Bill Clinton was governor twice, first in 1979 and then again in 1983, with Governor Frank White in-between) that not only cover what the governors and their families ate but show what it was like to work for them. The book is also illustrated with items from the mansion's dining rooms, as well as photographs of Chef Liza Ashley and the folks she served.

It's in this book that I came across several pie recipes, such as Gov. Francis Cherry's favored pecan pie and lemon cheese tarts. Two other recipes, for Gov. David Pryor's blueberry torte and Clinton's favorite lemon chess pie, appear in this book. It's in Ashley's collection where she shares that, while she worked for Governor Cherry, it was under Governor Orval Faubus that she became cook. One of the first dishes she made for Faubus and subsequent governors was this biscuit-topped pie. Technically, it has no bottom crust so lacks the real pie designation, but I'll allow it here. The recipe is adapted because chickens are three times larger today than they were in the 50s.

1/2 chicken or 3 pounds bone-in chicken thighs	1 bay leaf
3 cups water	1/2 cup flour
1 medium onion, chopped	1-2/3 cup evaporated milk
1 handful celery tops	2 cups cooked, sliced carrots
1 teaspoon salt	1 pound small white onions, cooked
1/4 teaspoon pepper	6-8 uncooked biscuits of choice

Put first seven ingredients in a stockpot and simmer for 2 hours or until tender. Remove chicken from broth. Strain broth and reserve. Remove meat from bones in large pieces and reserve. Refrigerate broth and meat separately, so schmaltz (chicken fat) can be harvested.

Heat fat in saucepan. Blend in flour to begin a roux, then add broth and evaporated milk. Cook, stirring constantly, until broth thickens, then boil one minute.

Add chicken, carrots and small onions. Add seasoning if needed. Heat through. Pour into a three quart baking dish and top with biscuits. Bake at 450° for 20-25 minutes.

CHICKEN PIE

In my quest to find the perfect chicken pie recipe, I came across this version in the 1981 edition of *Alpena Cooks*, contributed by Carol Woolston.

What I found here was, just like my first attempts at the Orval Faubus chicken pie recipe, was that the size of chickens today changes the recipe.

See, chickens in the mid-50s weighed an average of 3.07 pounds. In 2026, that weight was 6.18 pounds - those numbers coming from the National Chicken Council. So a recipe from 1950 will only need half a chicken, and a recipe from 1981 is somewhere in-between.

This is a good pie, don't get me wrong, else it would not be here. But it was just another step in my search. When it calls for adding more salt and pepper to taste, consider other spices such as parsley, garlic salt, or sage to enhance the flavor.

1/2 fryer chicken or 4 pounds bone-in chicken
1 large carrot, cut small
1 Tablespoon cornstarch or flour
3 chicken bouillon cubes
salt and pepper to taste
3 or 4 potatoes, cut small
1 frozen package or 1 small can peas
1 medium onion, chopped
2 unbaked 9 inch pie crusts

Boil the chicken in just enough water to cover. When it's done, remove from water and cool.

Put all remaining ingredients except for crust into broth and cook until vegetables are tender.

Pull chicken from the bone and cut small. Add to pot. Cook a few more minutes, uncovered, adding salt and pepper to taste.

Shake cornstarch or flour in 1/4 cup water until smooth. Add to pot and stir over heat until broth thickens.

Prepare 3 quart casserole or deep dish pie plate with one of the crusts. Spoon filling into crust, then add top crust, crimp and seal.

Vent pie and bake at 350° until top crust is golden brown, about 30 minutes. Let sit 20 minutes before serving, to allow the broth and crust to settle together.

Savory Pies

The Great Arkansas Pie Book

CHICKEN SCHMALTZ PIE

After going through 11 different recipes through the decades of cookbooks I've been digging into, working through all those different crusts, reading and just processing dozens of pounds of chicken, I think I came up with the ultimate chicken pie recipe. The secret - using chicken and seasoning every step along the way.

To start, let's talk about that crust. It's based on a 19th century recipe which calls for schmaltz - rendered chicken fat. Instead of boiling chicken, I roast it with salt, pepper, sage, and thyme, then refrigerate the pan drippings. The cold fat rises to the top and can be removed in a disc. That's the schmaltz.

Roasting also leaves behind aspic, the "meat jelly" you find in the bottom of your leftovers pan when you roast and then refrigerate chicken. I take it and the rest of the pan drippings and put it in a pot with veggie scraps - celery ends and tops, a handful of leftover carrots, and some outer onion layers that seemed a bit tough. I also remove the meat from the chicken bones and toss the bones in the pot, too. I boil this down into a thick aspic stock I use instead of water or milk as the liquid in my pie,

Savory Pies

seasoning the meat, seasoning the broth, and tasting every step of the way. Doing all of this takes a little extra time, but no part of the bird goes to waste. The aspic stock, schmaltz, and pan drippings I don't use are frozen for later, and work in so many ways (like using chicken fat in this crust for the rabbit pie on page 257). Almost any vegetable scraps can be used in the broth, too. These are things our grandparents and their grandparents would have done to subsist centuries ago, and they produce tasty results.

Schmaltz crust

- 12.5 ounces all purpose flour
- 1 teaspoons coarse salt
- 1 1/3 cup schmaltz, cold
- Up to 1/2 cup cold water
- More schmaltz for glazing between layers

In a food processor, pulse together 2/3rds of the flour and salt. Chunk schmaltz into pea sized pieces and place over surface. Pulse together ~20 times until dough looks like small crumbs. Add remaining four and pulse five more times. Turn out into bowl. Sprinkle with water and press into a ball. Divide in half and refrigerate one hour.

Before making the filling, you will need

- 5 pounds chicken parts of choice, bone-in, skin on
- 1/2 teaspoon sage
- 1/2 teaspoon thyme
- 1/2 teaspoon salt
- 1/4 teaspoon black pepper
- 2 cups vegetable trimmings (celery tops, carrots, onion, scallions, turnips, spinach, or any other flavorful vegetables) or 1/2 cup carrots, chopped
- 1/2 cup onions, chopped
- 1/2 cup celery, chopped

Heat oven to 350°. Place chicken on a rack in a large roasting pan or casserole. Mix seasonings together and dust chicken. Roast in oven for one hour, or until skin is crispy and chicken has reached an internal temperature of 165°. Take pan out of oven. Lift chicken on rack out and set to side. Drain drippings into 1 quart measuring cup. Remove chicken from bones and reserve both chicken and bones. Refrigerate all overnight.

The next day, take chicken drippings out of the refrigerator. Remove the schmaltz from the top and set aside. Put the remainder of the drippings in a pot to simmer, along with the chicken bones and vegetables. Let simmer away on the back of the

The Great Arkansas Pie Book

stove at least two hours while you work on other things. Add water to cover, if necessary. Do not let scorch. Strain out all solids and reserve this aspic broth in the fridge until ready to use.

Filling
2-1/2 cups chicken reserved from roasting
1 Tablespoon schmaltz or butter
1/2 cup onion, diced
1 Tablespoon flour
1/4 teaspoon salt
1 large package or 2 cans assorted vegetables of choice

Taste and season chicken, if it needs more seasoning. Chop. Set aside.

In the bottom of a stockpot, saute the onion in the schmaltz or butter until translucent. Add the flour and stir into the fat quickly, to make a roux. As soon as the flour is completely incorporated into the fat, pour in the broth slowly, whisking all the way. Add salt and vegetables and cook until broth thickens. If you'd like a thicker broth, you can add 1 teaspoon cornstarch or 1 teaspoon flour stirred into a quarter cup water at this time.

Add chicken once broth has thickened. Bring to a bubbling boil, and allow the filling to reduce to desired thickness. Remove from heat.

Heat oven to 350°. Roll out dough thin, use pastry brush to glaze with a little schmaltz, fold over and roll to 2 inches larger than pie plate. Lay into deep dish pie pan, trimming to an inch around outside of edge. Patch any holes with trimmings.

Spoon filling into crust. Do not overfill - any additional filling can be reserved for other use. Fold in edges of bottom crust. Repeat roll, brush and fold with second crust and lay over top. Cut crust to an inch over the edge all the way around, then tuck it under between the bottom crust and the pie plate. Glaze with egg wash if desired. Bake 30-35 minutes or until top crust is golden.

Savory Pies

LAYERED VEGETABLE PARMESAN PIE

Nancy Bryant contributed this recipe to *Concerts in the Kitchen* by the Arkansas Symphony Orchestra back in 1980. I found adding some grated Parmesan to the crust enhanced the flavor.

1 pastry crust shell (butter or olive oil crust works well)
6 Tablespoons grated Parmesan cheese
1 medium eggplant, quartered and thinly sliced
1 medium onion, thinly sliced
2 small or 1 large zucchini, thinly sliced
1 green bell pepper, thinly sliced
2 small or 1 large yellow squash, thinly sliced
2 medium tomatoes, seeded and thinly sliced
4 Tablespoons olive oil
1/2 teaspoon crushed garlic

Lay crust into pie plate and sprinkle with two tablespoons Parmesan. Bake five minutes at 350° until pastry crust starts to tan. Set aside.

Separately saute zucchini, onions, and green bell pepper in as little olive oil as possible and set aside. Layer pie beginning with zucchini slices, sprinkling cheese between each layer.

Mix remaining olive oil and garlic together and drizzle over top of pie. Scatter top with remaining Parmesan. Bake at 350° for 40-45 minutes or until vegetables are tender.

> **Fritos Chili Pie**
>
> 2½ cups Frito corn chips
> 1 large onion
> 1 cup grated cheese
> 1 15 oz chili
>
> Put 1½ cups Fritos in baking dish, arrange chopped onion & ½ grated cheese over Fritos. Pour heated chili over this & top with remaining Fritos & cheese. Bake 10 min 350°

Technically not a pie, this recipe, found in a notebook at Goodwill, is for Frito Chili Pie. The dish may have been created in 1957 by Claude Spradlin of the Dairy De-Lite in England, Arkansas.

MINCEMEAT PIE

Another gem once offered at the venerable Heights facility of Sue Lopez, and still as good. This is a true mincemeat, with your choice of beef or pork in the filling.

1 pound lean ground pork (can use beef)
1/2 teaspoon salt
1 cup brown sugar
1 teaspoon ground cinnamon
1/2 teaspoon ground cloves
5 cups apple juice
1-1/2 cups grape juice
1-1/2 cups orange juice
1 cup raisins
1 cup candied fruit
1/2 cup chopped pecans
1 cup crushed pineapple
5 to 6 (9-inch) unbaked pie shells and tops
Granulated sugar, for sprinkling

Crumble pork (or beef) into a large pan and cook with salt until done. Add remaining ingredients (except pie shells and granulated sugar) and mix well. Simmer 3 hours. Cool and then refrigerate until ready to use. Keeps very well.

For pies: Put mincemeat in pie shell. Make slits in tops and place on pie. Seal edges and sprinkle with sugar. Bake at 400° for 10 minutes, then at 350° for 10 to 15 minutes or until crust is done. This is enough filling for up to six pies.

MRS. MILLER'S CHICKEN POT PIE

The famed chicken and steak house that once graced Hot Springs may be long gone, but its reputation remains. It was in its heyday known not just for magnificent steaks but also chicken livers and fried chicken, roasted quail and lobster tail. And its chicken pot pie remains embedded in the memories of generations of diners.

In 1987, this recipe for the delicacy was shared in *Historic Hot Springs Collections* by Judy Giddings and June Simmons,.

This is a "handed-down" recipe, for the original Mrs. Miller didn't use exact measurements for any of it. Prepare your own favorite pie crust recipe. Line individual oven-proof serving bowls with crust to the top. Bake shells until golden brown. Remove from oven. Cut up and boil a hen, reserving broth. Remove meat from bones; chop into bite-size pieces. Mix reserve broth with flour and salt and pepper to taste. Cook over low heat until thick. Add chopped meat. Pour into pie shells; serve hot. Any left over meat mixture may be frozen for later use. Serve with candied carrots.

Savory Pies

MUFFALETTA PIE

There are a lot of great historic savory pie recipes... and then there's a whole new cadre of new ones, too, like this south Louisiana inspired pie from Abigail Eaves

2 unbaked 9 inch pastry pie crusts
8 ounces provalone cheese, sliced or shredded
8 ounces deli ham, sliced
8 ounces deli turkey, sliced
Muffaletta olive spread, well-drained

Heat oven to 425°.

Lay bottom crust into cast iron skillet or deep dish pie pan. Layer in the cheese, meats, and olive spread in alternating layers until the pan is filled.

Place top crust, trim and crimp to form a tight lid; make sure to cut slits in the crust.

Bake for 30 minutes. Allow to set before serving.

MUSHROOM PIE

My longtime hobby, participating in medieval re-creation in the Society for Creative Anachronism, has given me the chance to dive deep into many food cultures of the past. Over three decades, I've created 15 different feasts and a host of lunches, dinners and nibbles based on research into the cuisine of dozens of places and times.

I suppose it's fitting, then, that some of those dishes have come into my usual round of foods. This particular mushroom pie recipe, a longtime favorite, was redacted from the 14th century cookbook *Le Menagier de Paris*.

2 pounds mushrooms of choice
2 Tablespoons olive oil
3 Tablespoons Worcestershire
1 clove garlic, finely sliced
1/2 cup Parmesan cheese
1 cup Mozzarella cheese
2 unbaked 9 inch pastry pie crusts
salt and pepper to taste

In a large skillet, heat olive oil over medium-low. Gently wash mushrooms and slice. Saute garlic for one minute, then add mushrooms and fold into pan, covering with the oil. Pour Worcestershire sauce onto mushrooms and fold again. Saute until mushrooms become soft. Remove from heat and fold in cheeses. Let cool.

Heat oven to 350°. Lightly grease pie pan. Lay in bottom crust. Scoop mushroom mixture into pie pan. Press on top crust. Bake for 30-35 minutes. Allow to sit 10 minutes before serving.

MUSHROOM SOUR CREAM PIE

Brooks Robinson, the longtime third baseman for the Baltimore Orioles, hails from Little Rock. He is generally considered to have been the greatest defensive third baseman in major league history. This is his recipe, and it originally appeared in the 1980 *Calico Cupboards* cookbook by the Benton Junior Auxiliary.

1 baked 9 inch pastry pie crust
1 pound fresh mushrooms
3 Tablespoons butter
1/2 cup chopped onion
3 eggs
1 cup sour cream
1 teaspoon salt
1/2 teaspoon tarragon leaves
dash pepper
1/4 cup shredded Swiss cheese

Preheat oven to 350°. In skillet, saute mushrooms and onion in butter. In medium bowl beat eggs, sour cream, salt, tarragon and pepper. Pour mixture into mushroom and onion mixture and pour into pie shell. Top with cheese. Bake for 30 minutes or until golden.

Savory Pies

ONION PIE

The Arkansas Division of the American Cancer Society included this savory pie recipe in its 1992 cookbook, *Arkansas Heritage: Recipes Past and Present*. I have determined that, when I made this pie, I like to crush an additional cup of crackers and lay them over the first layer before adding the filling. This alleviates dampness you get when this pie sits overnight. It's not necessary otherwise, and I'll point out that the original recipe called it to be served immediately.

1 cup finely crushed crackers
1/4 cup melted butter
2 cups finely sliced onions
2 Tablespoons butter
2 eggs
3/4 cup milk
3/4 teaspoon salt
Pepper to taste
1/4 cup Cheddar cheese
Paprika to taste

Mix crackers and butter in a bowl. Press into 8 inch pie plate. Saute onions in butter until transparent. Spoon into prepared pie plate. Combine eggs, milk, salt, and pepper in a bowl; mix well. Pour over onions. Sprinkle with cheese and paprika. Bake at 350° for 30 minutes or until set. Garnish with parsley if desired. Serve immediately.

Savory Pies

PASTRAMI PASTRAMI REUBEN PIE

Ken Dempsey likes making savory things happen, particularly when it comes to pies. He's managed to win The Root Cafe's Pie-Off a couple different times with pies that defy the sweet standard to showcase savory selections. While this sandwich-inspired pie didn't take the top prize, it still got a rousing cheer from me.

Layer the following over a pre-baked bottom pie crust in order:
2 cups sour cream and chive mashed potatoes
1/2 cup shredded provolone
1/2 pound sliced pastrami
1/4 cup Thousand island dressing
1 cup Bulgarian kraut
1/2 cup shredded provolone
1 unbaked 9 inch pastry pie crust

Bake pie at 385° for 30 minutes. Broil three minutes or more, until crust is golden brown.

RABBIT PIE

First week of January 2023, I'm digging into more cookbooks from the myriad of boxes I brought with me to Writers' Colony, waiting for pies to come out of both the top and bottom ovens and aching to fill any gaps in pie making I felt I needed to cover. I'm about a third of a way into one of the boxes and find a small yellow stapled book with a familiar font.

The book, *Boilin' N' Bakin' In Booger Hollow*, instantly takes me back to those stops made as a child, a teenager, and even a young college student at this spot in the road called Booger Hollow - "population 7, counten' one coon dog" - alongside Scenic Arkansas Highway Seven north of Dover. Now, let me express to you about this place, this magical tourist attraction, one of dozens that lined our rural Ozark highways when I was young. The Arkansas aesthetic, the deep-in-the-Ark-en-saw talk, the Arkan-speak of severely over-pronounced hillbilly dialect, was a big draw when I was a kid. Our backwoods state could be proud of our rural heritage, and the fact that Al Capp chose to place his Dogpatch USA theme park in the heart of the hollows about an hour's drive north was not lost. Folks would stop in for postcards, round tuits, wooden hatchet-hewn furniture, vittles, smoked ham and fudge, and a photo opportunity next to a, I kid you not, double decker outhouse.

Booger Hollow Trading Post became a pit stop, along with Rotary Ann and Scenic Point, on that windy tight road that took you into the stereotypical Ozark landscape. I have vague memories of a 1991 television package that tied then-governor Bill Clinton, running for president, to the hokey yet endearing red-and-white painted edifice and its homespun appeal.

I remember stopping in with family members when I was in my single digits and when I was in high school. During my four years at Arkansas Tech University, I often sought the curves of Highway Seven for a quick drive all the way to Harrison and back, not because Harrison had all that much to offer, but because I could, and stops at Dogpatch USA and the Jasper town square and Booger Hollow were common.

Though the theme park closed about the time I graduated, and though I moved across state shortly thereafter for my first TV job, a visit back to the alma mater or to my boyfriend's dad's place in Dardanelle often included the quick jaunt to Booger Hollow, for the hell of it.

Come 2007, and at the age of 33 I made the big jump from being a television producer to scratching out a living as a writer. I knew the sort of stories I wanted to tell, and a big one of those stories was that of Booger Hollow. So imagine my dismay one foggy October day to make it all the way up there from Little Rock, only to find the front door locked and an air of abandonment about the place. Me, with my sense of investigation about me, walked around and right inside through a door left open. The story I wrote about it, "Ghosts of Booger Hollow," would first appear on my Tie Dye Travels website, then in a few local papers, and earn me the dubious distinction of being the top search result on Google for the word BOOGER for several years.

Booger Hollow never came back, but this cookbook did come to me, and holding the tiny yellow tome, complete with its handwritten scrawl in Arkan-speak and a smattering of illustrations, I decided it was worth a dive. I quickly made up its version of chess pie, found it good, and about put it back before something told me to give it a quick cover-to-cover read. That's when I found the rabbit pie recipe.

RUPERT'S RABBIT PIE

1 dead rabbit
4 slices fried bakon
1 teaspoon chopped parsley
2 sliced boiled aigs
1 onion

dash pepper
1/2 teaspoon salt
pie crust
pincha sage

Undress rabbit 'n baithe hit. Take the meat offin' the bones 'n soak in cold water... drain. Put in a pan, cover wid water 'n boil fur bout 15 min. wid salt, pepper 'n onion, then put in pie pan wid bakon, parsley, aigs, sage 'n sum stock. Kiver wid pie crust n' bake for an hour at 375°. Whilst this is a 'cookin go out 'n set the rabbit trap agin'.

I chuckled over it. I posted it to Facebook for a good laugh, with an inch of doubt that it was a real recipe. When asked why I didn't tackle it, I admitted that my recollection of rabbit is that, like duck, wild harvested has an entirely different flavor to it than farm raised. After all, Arkansas is home to Pel-Freez, the world's largest rabbit meat producer, so getting a domestic rabbit would not be hard. This sort of recipe, though, required something more, and I was satisfied to give that answer and move on.

My friend Jason Kennedy, though, he was more than willing to oblige my experimentation. He let me know he had a wild-harvested rabbit in his freezer that he'd be glad to give me, in the name of research. I was daunted but I collected the hare, packed my bags in February and made another jaunt to Writers' Colony.

I made dozens and dozens and dozens of pies that second stint, first for the pie talk I gave to a hungry, happy crowd,

and second to fill the final gaps in my research for this very book. Each day I'd consider the rabbit, and I even got to a point a few days before my time was done to thaw it and begin the process of removing it from its bones and soaking it in milk. But every time I went to begin the filling, I got the heebie jeebies and went on to something else.

That's how I came, at 2 a.m. on a Friday morning, to find myself faced with the ready-to-go rabbit as I cleaned the Culinary Suite kitchen. I had by this point worked through almost all of my flour, having made so many crusts and working through so much schmaltz. I was to the dregs of my vegetables and I'd already given the countertops a good scouring. I should have been done.

Nay. Nay, I say, I needed to get past my cooking block and make this little dish. So I did, taking the soaked rabbit and throwing him into his filling, bringing chicken schmaltz together with a bit of the rabbit drippings and seasoning to press together a crust, rolling out six translucent sheets of pastry, setting three layers into a handmade ceramic pie pot, spooning in the filling and sealing it once, twice, thrice over in more layers of dough pierced through and tucked under at the edge. I lovingly washed its top with egg and slid it into the oven, set my alarm and went to bed, and almost left it to burn away.

The scent of this pie, though, through from the kitchen through the dining room and into the sleeping quarters roused me a good five minutes before the alarm would have sounded. I gingerly pulled out the dish, peered at it, and thought I was dreaming

This, my friends, is what I had wrought - a recipe I had thought might be purely whimsical, packed with translucent onions and spice and tiny pieces of rabbit, that crust flaking apart as I pulled its first slice. I took my photos with the assumption that on first tasting I'd be back in the kitchen, trying to figure out the true spice ratio, needing to make it all right. But it was... all right. It was more than all right. It was just as worthy a dish as any I have encountered in my travels, worthy just as much of being served on fine china in an elevated restaurant as being scooped out of a Dutch oven on a cold winter's night.

I impart to you, then, this humble recipe I have with my own mouth tasted, for rabbit pie.

Savory Pies

RABBIT PIE

Two pastry pie crusts
   (schmaltz-made on page 241
   or lard-made crust is preferred)
1 whole wild-harvested rabbit
Milk to cover rabbit
1/2 teaspoon salt
dash pepper
1 medium onion, sliced
1 Tablespoon butter
4 slices bacon, fried & crumbled
2 boiled eggs, sliced
1 teaspoon chopped fresh parsley
pinch sage
1 cup rendered aspic stock
   or broth of choice

Debone rabbit, reserving bones to make stock if desired. Cube meat, place in bowl, cover with milk and refrigerate for at least two hours. Drain. Season with salt and pepper.

Saute rabbit and onion together in butter. Add 1/2 cup stock and bring to a boil, stirring occasionally, for 15 minutes. Remove from heat.

Take one of the pastry doughs, fold in half twice, and roll out to cover 8- or 9-inch pie plate (or cut and roll out dough thin to layer into bottom of pan). Layer in half of rabbit and onion mix, sage, bacon crumbles, sliced eggs, and remainder of rabbit mix. Fold and roll second crust twice, lay across top of pie plate, trim edges to one inch and tuck under the lower crust. Brush with egg wash if desired.

Bake at 375° for one hour. Let set at least 20 minutes before serving.

SPANIKOPITA

Spinach pie... that's what spanikopita happens to be. Yes, indeed, it's also a pastry on its own sometimes, but the only difference is the vessel in which it is cooked. The dish is here because of its uniquely Arkansas connection - this is the recipe used for spanikopita at the annual International Greek Food Festival, held at Little Rock's Annunciation Greek Orthodox Church.

3 packages (10 ounces each) chopped frozen spinach
1-1.5 cups onion, chopped
1/2 cup butter or olive oil
1/2 cup green onion, chopped
1 Tablespoon dill weed
1/4 cup fresh parsley

5 eggs, slightly beaten
1 pound feta cheese, crumbled
salt, to taste
white pepper, to taste
1 pound filo dough, defrosted
1 cup clarified butter, melted

Thaw spinach, drain and squeeze out most of the moisture.

In large, heavy pot or Dutch oven, sauté onions in butter; add green onions, dill weed and parsley and stir. Remove from heat. Allow to cool for 10 minutes. Add eggs, cheese, salt and pepper to onion mixture..

Preheat oven to 350°. Butter a 9 x 13" pan. Remove filo from package and lay on flat surface. Layer bottom and sides of pan with one sheet of filo, then brush with clarified butter. Continue layering for 10 sheets, brushing each sheet with butter.

Spread spinach filling evenly over filo layers in pan. Fold edges of filo over spinach. Place remaining filo over filling, brushing each sheet with butter, and trim excess filo around pan.

Score tip of pie with sharp knife to mark squares. Bake on bottom rack for 40-50 minutes or until golden brown. Cut and serve hot or cold.

Savory Pies

SPINACH MUSHROOM PIE

This pie recipe submitted by Evelyn Ward is listed as a spinach quiche in the 1977 cookbook *RX Prepare as Directed and Enjoy* by the Baptist Medical Center Arkansas Rehabilitation Institute Auxiliary. It doesn't actually include eggs. I did put it in my eleventh book, *Arkansas Cookery: Retro Recipes from The Natural State* - it's just really good and worthy of inclusion here.

1 unbaked 9 inch pastry pie crust
1 small onion, diced
2 Tablespoons butter or oleo
1-4 ounce can mushrooms
3/4 pound Swiss or Feta cheese
2 packages frozen spinach

Saute onion in butter. Add mushrooms, cheese and spinach. Fold into unbaked pie crust. Bake at 350° for an hour.

SPINACH PARMESAN PIE

This recipe from Bettie Ann Mahony is in the cookbook *In Good Taste* by the El Dorado Service League from 1980. It's a meal in a pie.

Pastry
3 eggs
1/2 cup butter, melted
1 Tablespoon oil
1/4 cup dry skim milk solids
2 cups all-purpose flour
1 teaspoon baking powder
1 teaspoon salt
1/2 teaspoon nutmeg

Filling
1 - 10 ounce package spinach, steamed and chopped
2 eggs, beaten
1 cup heavy cream
1-3/4 cups fresh grated Parmesan
1-6 ounce can pitted black olives
1/2 Bermuda onion, sliced and sauteed
1/2 teaspoon nutmeg

Beat eggs in mixer until thick and pale yellow. Add butter and oil slowly. Gradually add remaining pastry ingredients in order listed. Turn dough out onto pastry board. Knead until a uniform dough is reached, about five minutes. Roll out to fit a 9 inch buttered pie plate.

Heat oven to 350°. Combine all ingredients for filling and pour into pastry shell. Bake for 30 minutes. Garnish with watercress.

TAMALE PIE

A very simple and quick dinner pie recipe found in several Arkansas cookbooks of the 1980s.

1 package Mexican cornbread mix
2/3 cup milk
1 egg, beaten

1 can tamales
1 can chili
8 ounces shredded Cheddar

Stir together cornbread mix, milk and egg. Pour into 9x13 casserole dish, making sure to push mix up the sides. In a separate bowl, mix together tamales and chili. Pour on top of cornbread mix. Top with cheese. Bake at 375° until edge of cornbread is golden brown, 20-30 minutes.

Savory Pies

TURKEY POT PIE

Looking for an easy savory pie filling? This poultry filling is made in the CrockPot while you do other things - like, I don't know, make more pie crusts? It's also a good way to use post-Thanksgiving leftovers.

- 3 cups cooked turkey or chicken, chopped
- 2 cups turkey broth from pan or 2 cans broth
- 1 cup water
- 1 cup each diced carrots, onions and celery or one 12 ounce bag mirepoix frozen mix
- 1 bay leaf
- 1 can sliced potatoes
- 1 can corn
- 1 can green beans
- 1 cup milk
- 1 cup flour
- 2 teaspoons poultry seasoning
- 1 teaspoon white pepper
- 1 teaspoon black pepper
- 1 teaspoon salt
- 2 unbaked 9 inch pastry pie crusts

Set CrockPot to low. Combine in CrockPot the broth, water, mirepoix, bay leaf, and turkey. Add pepper(s), salt and poultry seasoning. Stir well. Add potatoes, corn and green beans *and the liquid in the cans.*

Make a slurry with the milk and flour and add it to the CrockPot. Stir all well. Cook on low 7-9 hours (overnight works well). Remove bay leaf. Allow to cool completely before serving or baking.

To bake: Heat oven to 350° degrees. Spray or wipe down two deep dish pie plates or one 3 quart or larger casserole dish. Line dish(es) with pie dough and blind bake for 10 minutes. Remove from oven. Add in pot pie filling, cover with remaining crust and bake for 35-45 minutes. Remove from oven and allow to sit for at least 10 minutes before serving.

ZUCCHINI PIE

A nice meatless pie suitable for a side dish. This version comes from *Variety Pack: Favorite Recipes of the Friends of the MS Society and St. Bernard's, Volume II* from 2000, and was contributed by Terry A. Wren.

3 cups unpeeled zucchini, cubed
4 eggs
1 medium onion
1 cup biscuit mix
1/4 cup olive oil
2 Tablespoons parsley flakes
1/4 teaspoon pepper
1/4 teaspoon salt
1/2 cup grated Romano or Parmesan cheese

Mix all ingredients. Spray a deep 10 inch pie pan with a small amount of oil or cooking spray and turn mix into pan. Bake at 350° for 45 minutes, until top is lightly brown. Cool for five minutes and serve.

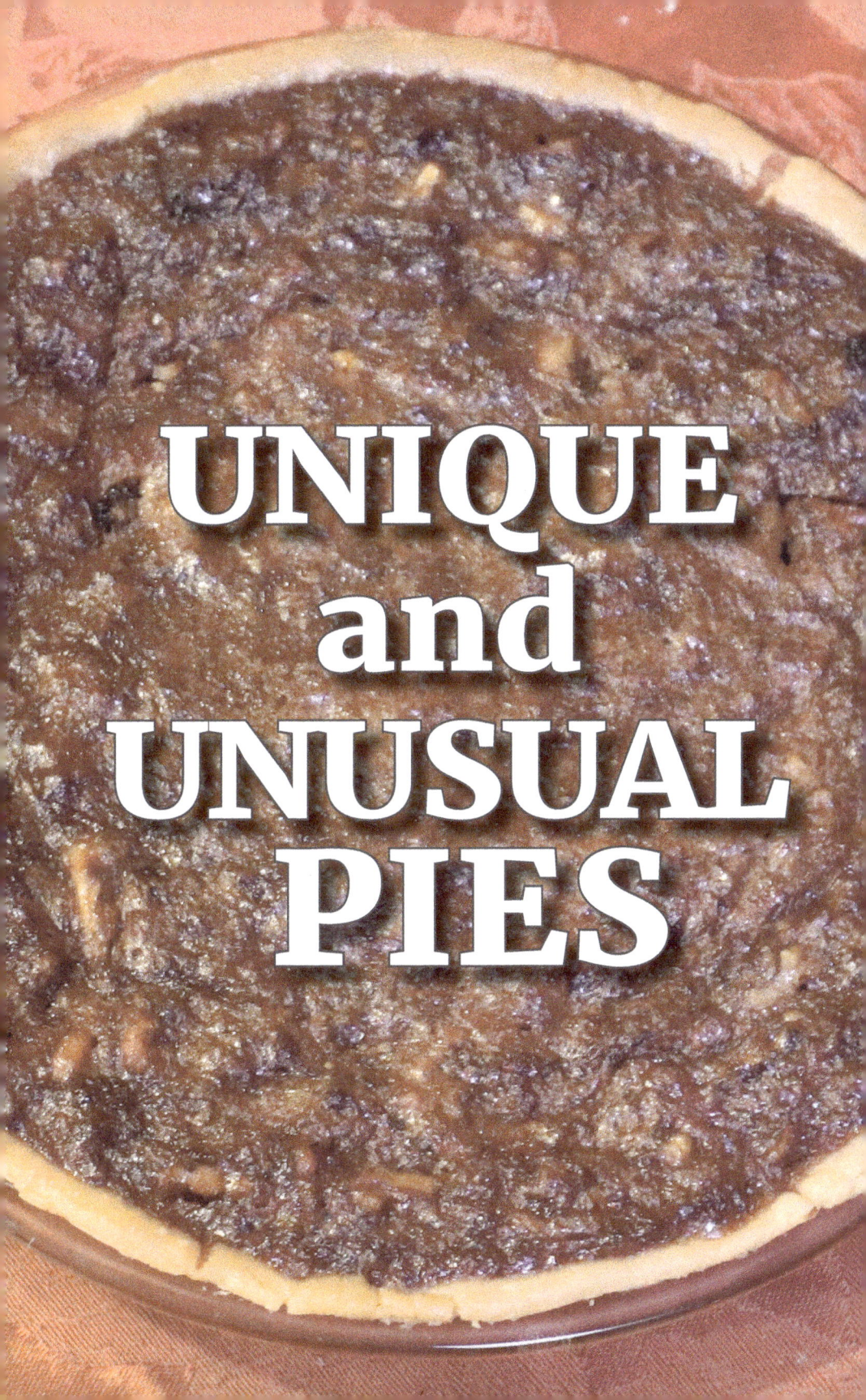

UNIQUE and UNUSUAL PIES

COMPANY'S COMIN' PIE

This singular pie has, for decades, been offered at the Cliff House Inn, some six miles south and 1100 feet above the Jasper town square. It has on various materials been listed as the state pie of Arkansas. Don't get me wrong - it's a good pie, but that's not the case.

Back in 1986, Arkansas celebrated its sesquicentennial - its first 150 years since statehood in 1836. There were a whole slew of cookbooks that came out about this time, promoted by the Arkansas Sesquicentennial Committee. There were public events of all sorts, and then-governor Bill Clinton made a lot of neat pronouncements. One of those was for the Pie of the Arkansas Sesquicentennial - to which, he named the lofty, airy, and very sweet Company's Comin' Pie, specifically that served at the Cliff House Inn in Jasper.

Now, I've found recipes in quite a few cookbooks of the 1970s and 1980s, including *Cornerstone Cookery*, the 1985 cookbook from St. Vincent's Infirmary that my mom, Kitty Waldon, put together. The specific recipe, though, I was given during a conversation with Becky McLaurin back in August 2012, while I was working on my first book, *Arkansas Pie: A Delicious Slice of The Natural State*. She keyed me in on the history of the restaurant and the pie.

The Cliff House Inn was opened in 1967, and over the years has seen several owners. In the middle, there were Bob and Francis McDaniel, who held the property over an 18 year span. Francis

Unique and Unusual Pies

wanted the restaurant to gain note, so worked to create a couple of signature dishes, in particular a light and sweet fluffy biscuit and a particular, unique pie.

"Francis tried different pies and hit on it, because people would call ahead and ask 'you know that pie you make? The one with the pineapple?'" Becky told me. "'We're heading that way and wanted to make sure you had it.'" Hence the name of the pie she stuck with, Company's Comin' Pie.

No other Arkansas restaurant offers this pie on its regular menu - probably because it's not a simple pie to make, thanks to its meringue crust.

"The pie crust is sorta like a Divinity crust," McLaurin told me, "made with egg whites and sugar. It takes about an hour to make a pie crust. You beat the egg whites and the sugar for about 25 minutes, and then you add crushed saltine crackers and a cup of pecan pieces, and then you stir that in and it's kinda like a thick gooey mixture. You take and divide it into two pie tins. You form the crust with a spatula and bake it for 25 minutes.

"When you get ready to serve a pie, you take a pint of real whipping cream and put a little sugar in, and then you add a bit of crushed pineapple. Fill your pie crust with that. It's kind of an unusual pie but people love it."

The McDaniels would go on to sell the restaurant to Jim Berry. Now, Berry was active in the tourism community, and when the word got out that the theme of the 1986 tourism campaign was going to be "Company's Comin', Let's Get Ready," he had a suggestion - why not tie the oddly named Company's Comin' Pie to the festivities? And that's how the pie got its recognition, thanks to Jim Berry and Bill Clinton.

But there's never been an official declaration for the pie of Arkansas. I did, in that same *Arkansas Pie* book, make a case that the true state pie of Arkansas should be the possum pie, also known as Four Layer Delight and Sex in a Pie Pan. I based my decision at the time on the prevalence of the dish throughout the entire state, and indeed, in 2019, *People Magazine* named the Arkansas Possum Pie at Tusk and Trotter in Bentonville as the best pie in the entire state (for that recipe, see page 170). Still, the legislature has never determined a state pie or even a state dessert.

Regardless, there is no pie like the Company's Comin' Pie at the Cliff House Inn. It is sweet and effervescent, and only available in the warmer months when the restaurant is open. Go enjoy a slice while looking out on the Arkansas Grand Canyon - or make this version for yourself.

Crust
6 egg whites
1 teaspoon cream of tartar
2 cups sugar
1 teaspoon vanilla
1 sleeve saltine crackers, crushed
1/2 cup chopped pecans

Topping
1 small container whipped topping
3 Tablespoons sugar
2 Tablespoons crushed pineapple

Beat egg whites until fluffy. Add cream of tartar and sugar. Beat 25 minutes or until stiff. Stir in vanilla. Stir in crackers and pecans by hand. Spray two pie pans with nonstick spray. Divide mixture evenly between pans. Spread mixture in pan, forming a crust. Bake at 285° degrees for 25 minutes or until done. Combine topping ingredients. Pour into pie shell. Serve and enjoy.

Unique and Unusual Pies

DOG TICK PIE

It may not sound that appetizing, but this is just another type of raisin pie. The raisins blow up and look like those big ticks you see swoll up on old hound dogs that spend their days running the woods of rural Arkansas, hence the name. Andrea Hensley's version comes from the 1986 book *Cooking Kin: The Favorite Recipes of the Jeffrey-Alexander Cousins*.

1-1/2 cups sugar
4 Tablespoons flour
1 egg, well beaten
3 Tablespoons lemon juice

2 teaspoons grated lemon rind
1/8 teaspoon salt
1 cup raisins
2 unbaked 9 inch pastry crusts

Blend sugar, flour, and egg together in a double-boiler. Add lemon juice, lemon rind, salt, and raisins and 2 cups water. Mix well. Cook until thick (about 15 minutes), stirring occasionally. Cool for 5 to 10 minutes. Poor into a 9" unbaked pie shell. Top with a lattice crust. Bake at 450° for 10 minutes. Reduce heat to 350° and bake for 20 more minutes or until browned.

FAWN PIE

A classic found in over a hundred Arkansas cookbooks, this is another variant on chess pie, with coconut and lemon for flavor. This version is from *Arkansas Cooking 1836-1986*, published by the Arkansas Sesquicentennial Committee It's attributed to Geraldine Parrish of Woodruff County Child Support Enforcement.

2 cups sugar
1 Tablespoon flour
1 Tablespoon cornmeal
1/2 teaspoon salt
1 teaspoon vanilla

1 stick butter, melted
4 eggs
3-1/2 ounces coconut flakes
1 - 8 ounce can crushed pineapple
2 unbaked 9 inch pastry pie crusts

Mix flour, sugar, cornmeal and salt. Add butter and beat until fluffy. Add eggs one at a time, beating well after each addition. Add undrained pineapple, coconut and vanilla. Stir well. Pour into pie shells and bake at 350 for 45-50 minutes, or until lightly browned.

FUNERAL PIE

It is a tradition in this neck of the woods, and elsewhere I'd also presume, that when a member of your family or community passes on, that those who remain are taken care of by others. In Arkansas, that means making sure the bereaved are housed and fed so they can concentrate on the other needs that may arrive. The announcement of a death is usually followed by an outpouring of support in the way of dishes delivered to the home. These often include casseroles both hot and ready and frozen to stick back and pull out when there's a need. It can be staple items such as breads or cookies, or it can be pie.

Funeral pie gets its name from this act of charity. It is a pie that's made from staples found in most any country kitchen. Once baked, it is stable and can sit on the counter a few days, which means very little care needs to be taken to make sure it stays good. Just cover it.

2 cups raisins
2 cups water
1/2 cup brown sugar
1/2 cup white sugar
1/2 teaspoon ground cinnamon
1/4 teaspoon ground allspice

pinch salt
3 Tablespoons cornstarch
1 Tablespoon apple cider vinegar
3 Tablespoons butter
2 unbaked 9 inch pastry pie crusts

Heat oven to 400°. Line a pie pan with one crust. Heat raisins in water in saucepan five minutes. Combine all dry ingredients and add to raisins. Allow to simmer another 5 minutes. Add vinegar and butter, and stir to combine. Let cool a little, pour into pie crust, top with other crust, vent, then bake 30-35 minutes or until golden brown.

GALAKTOBOUREKO

William Hronas shares this recipe for Greek Milk Pie from Marie Dunavan.

1 quart milk
3/4 cup farina cream of wheat or fine grain semolina
1 cup sugar
1 stick butter
2 teaspoons vanilla
6 eggs, separated
18 sheets fillo
clarified butter for the fillo

Syrup
1-1/2 cups sugar
1-1/2 cups water
Juice of half a lemon
1/4 cup Cointreau

Mix farina, milk, and sugar in pot. Add one stick butter and cook over low heat until thickened. Stir it constantly with whisk!! Set aside to cool, add vanilla. Add beaten egg yolks. Fold in stiffly beaten egg whites. Butter a 14x10 pan, lay and butter 8 fillo. Pour in mix, Layer 8-10 more fillo, buttering well between each. Put in fridge overnight.

To make the syrup, boil together the sugar, water and lemon juice. After boiling 10 minutes, add 1/4 cup Cointreau. Remove from heat and let cool.

Heat oven to 350°. Cut pastry and bake for one to one and a half hours or until golden brown . Pour cold syrup over hot pastry.

```
COCKTAIL PECAN PIE

1 3-oz. jar dried beef, chopped
1 8-oz. carton sour cream
1 8-oz. pkg. cream cheese, softened
1/2 cup finely minced green pepper
2 tsp. finely minced onion
1/4 tsp. garlic salt
1 cup chopped pecans
2 Tbsp. butter
Thoroughly combine beef, sour cream, cheese
green pepper, onion and garlic salt;
place in ovenproof casserole dish and top
with pecans sauteed in butter.
Bake at 350 deg. for 20 min.  Serve
with crackers or chips.  May be frozen.
Makes 10 to 12 servings.
```

The Great Arkansas Pie Book

GREEN TOMATO PIE

This is a recipe from Cornerstone Cookery,, attributed to Kitty Bear-Diemer. That's my mom. Funny thing is, when I made this recipe up back in 2020, we talked about it and she couldn't remember actually submitting this. It's... well, unique.

12 large green tomatoes, sliced
salt water
2 heaping Tablespoons butter
1 cup sugar
1/2 cup vinegar
1 teaspoon cinnamon
1 teaspoon nutmeg
1/2 teaspoon cloves
2 unbaked 9 inch pastry pie crusts

Boil tomatoes in weak salt water until well done; drain through colander. Stir in remaining ingredients and pour into pie shells. Bake at 350° for 30-35 minutes.

JAPANESE FRUIT PIE

This recipe comes from my aunt Beverly Sanders, who attributes it to her sister, Joyce Bear Parrish. It's both a Bear and Parrish family favorite at Christmas.

1 cup granulated sugar
2 eggs
1 stick margarine
1 Tablespoon vinegar
1/2 cup raisins
1/2 cup chopped pecans
1/2 cup sweetened coconut
1 deep dish 9 inch pastry pie shell

Preheat 350°.

(My sister said she does this part in the blender. ~ Beverly Sanders)
Using an electric mixer combine sugar, eggs, margarine and vinegar in a large mixing bowl. Add raisins, pecans and coconut to the mixture. Stir. Pour into unbaked pie crust. Cook 25 - 30 minutes. Cool.

This pie is very rich. Very easy to make.

JOY CHOY PIE

My friend Kelli Marks shared this pie from her grandmother's 1977 cookbook. It lands here because the ingredients are certainly an unusual combination!

1/2 cup crushed chow mein noodles (about 1 cup whole = 1/2 cup crushed)
3 egg whites
1/4 teaspoon cream of tartar
1 cup sugar
1 teaspoon vanilla extract
1/2 teaspoon lemon extract
1/2 cup chopped pecans
1 package frozen strawberries
1 cup heavy cream, whipped and chilled
1/4 cup confectioners' sugar

Beat egg whites and cream of tartar until almost stiff. Add sugar one tablespoon at a time while beating. Beat well after each addition. Add vanilla and lemon extracts. Beat until stiff peaks form. Fold in crushed noodles and crushed nuts.

Generously butter a 9 inch pie plate. Spread meringue in pan, making a hollow in the center, bring meringue up the sides of the pan. Bake at 350° for 30-35 minutes. Remove from heat and cool.

Fill center with partially thawed strawberries. Top with whipped cream sweetened with confectioners' sugar.

```
                Seaman's Pie

1 - 6 oz. pkg. noodles, cooked
1 - 7 oz. can tuna, drained
¼ cup onion, chopped
2 eggs, boiled and chopped
1 - 10 3/4 oz. can cream of mushroom soup
½ T. salt
Pepper to taste
1 teaspoon Worcestershire
Dash of Tabasco
1 T. parsley, chopped
¼ - ½ cup sharp cheese, grated

Put layer of noodles in square casserole.  Add
layer of tuna, onion and eggs.  Mix soup with
seasonings and pour over all.  Sprinkle cheese
on top.  Bake at 350° for 30 minutes.  Serves
4-6.

                             Betty Jones
```

OATMEAL PIE

A pecan pie without pecans? Indeed, this oatmeal pie is made in a similar fashion, and can be a good choice for folks who have a nut allergy. It's also an old subsistence-era pie that shows how inventive you can be when you don't have the ingredients you normally would use available. It comes from the Oark General Store.

3 eggs
1 cup brown sugar
1 cup corn syrup (Pride of Dixie brand preferred)
1-1/2 cup old-fashioned rolled oats
2 teaspoons vanilla extract
2 tablespoons melted salted butter
1 pie crust
1 unbaked 9 inch pastry pie crust

Preheat oven to 350°. Place uncooked pie crust into pie pan. Scatter the oats in the bottom, making sure to cover the bottom well (if you need a few extra oats, that's okay and will not affect outcome).

PCP PIE

After Alma French sold the old Ed and Kay's Restaurant, it was kept open by Ed and Kay Diemer, who ran it right up until 2014. Of all the pies, this pecan, coconut and pineapple was my favorite.

2 cups sugar
1 Tablespoon corn meal
1 Tablespoon flour
pinch of salt
5 eggs
1 cup pecans, coarsely chopped
1 cup drained crushed pineapple
1 cup flaked coconut
1 stick butter, melted
1 unbaked pie shell

Heat oven to 300°.

Fold together sugar, cornmeal, flour and salt. Beat eggs, then add dry ingredients and mix thoroughly. Stir in pecans, pineapple and coconut. Fold in melted butter. Pour into an unbaked pastry crust in a pie pan. Cover edges of crust with aluminum foil.

Bake 45-60 minutes or until pie is set. Cool before serving.

VINEGAR PIE

Vinegar pie has long been associated with Arkansas. The 19th century economy dessert was often utilized in the late days of winter, when the bounty of the farm was at its lowest and no fresh fruit or nuts were to be found. Its simplicity (similar to Chess Pie) was in how it created something unexpected from plain, ordinary ingredients.

From June 11, 1890, to April 15, 1891, Nannie Stillwell Jackson wrote about the best and meanest moments of her life on a small farm in southeast Arkansas. The University of Arkansas Press published that journal in 1982, under the title *Vinegar Pie and Chicken Bread: A Woman's Diary of Life in the Rural South, 1890-1891*.

- 4 large eggs
- 2 Tablespoons apple cider vinegar
- 1-1/2 cups sugar
- 1 stick unsalted butter, melted
- 1/2 teaspoon cinnamon
- 1 teaspoon vanilla
- 1 pinch salt
- 1 unbaked 9 inch pastry pie crust

Preheat oven to 425°. Beat eggs, vinegar, sugar, melted butter, cinnamon, vanilla, and salt until well combined and slightly thickened. Pour batter into pie crust and bake for 25 minutes. Center should be set. Cool before serving.

VINEGAR PIE

The Great Depression is cited as an engine for the creation of so many dishes that stretched a dime into a dollar - but that's not where the vinegar pie comes from. There are recipes that pre-date the Civil War for the extraordinarily simple dish. This version comes from Loretta Burns and is featured in *The Art of Cooking in Heber Springs*.

1 egg
2 Tablespoons flour
1 scant cup sugar
2 Tablespoons cider vinegar
1 cup cold water
dash nutmeg
1 augmented 9 inch pastry pie crust

Take pie crust and roll it out thick, tucking it into an 8-inch pie pan. Beat egg and flour together; add sugar and continue beating. Add vinegar and cold water. Cook on stovetop until thickened. Pour into pie shell and dust with nutmeg. Let stand an hour before serving.

RECIPES A-Z

18th Century Meat Pie 230
1829 Lemon Pie 28
All-Butter Pie Crust 21
Alligator Pie 86
Alma French's Chocolate Chess Pie 176
Alma French's Chocolate Meringue Pie 199
Alma French's Lemon Meringue Pie 205
Anderson's Restaurant Chocolate Pie 178
Anderson's Restaurant Egg Custard Pie 142
apple 29, 30, 35, 37, 40, 41, 43, 54, 57
Apple Pie 30
Apple Raisin Nut Pie 29
Arkansas Possum Pie 170
Arkansas's best source on food 284
Ashley at the Capital's Brown Sugar Pie 128
Bacon Fat Fried Pies 218
banana 86, 88, 89, 90, 152
Banana Pudding Pie 88
Banana Rum Pie 89
Banofee Pie 86
Basic Chocolate Pie 172
Beef Pie 250, 232
Beverly Sanders's Coconut Meringue Pie 202
Big Springs Trading Company's Buttermilk Pie 130
Bill Clinton's Favorite Lemon Chess Pie 149
Bittersweet Pie 173
Black and Blue Berry Pie 32
blackberry 60
Black Bottom Pie 174
Black Walnut Pie 66
blueberry 34, 90, 92, 124

Blueberry Banana Cream Pie 90
Blueberry Chess Pie 124
Blueberry Cream Pie 90
Blueberry Pie 34
Blueberry Strawberry Pie 33
Blueberry Torte 91
Blue Cake Honey Pies Cherry Mini Pies or Hand Pies 38
Blue Cake Honey Pies Pecan Pie 79
Bourbon Chocolate Chunk Pecan Pie 64
Bourbon Chocolate Pecan Pie 65
Bradley County Pink Tomato Pie 233
Brisket Pie 234
Brooks Robinson's Mushroom Sour Cream Pie 248
Brown Bag Apple Pie 35
Brown Sugar Buttermilk Pie 126
Brown Sugar Pecan Pie 68
Brown Sugar Pie 127, 128
Bubba's Sweet Potato Pie 162
Buffalo River Dining Hall Chocolate Meringue Pie 197
Burns Gables' Ozark Wild Huckleberry Pie 48
Burnt Sugar Pie 192
Buttermilk Pecan Pie 67
Buttermilk Pie 11, 130, 134
Cannoli Pie 132
caramel 36, 37, 68, 92, 112, 116, 192, 193
Caramel Bottom Peach Pie 36
Caramel Crunch Apple Pie 37
Caramel Nut Pie 68
Caramel Pecan Cream Cheese Pie 92
Caramel Pie 193
Cathie's Buttermilk Pie 134
Cheeseburger Pie 235
Cherries in the Snow 94
cherry 38, 39, 92, 94, 95, 96
Cherry Cream Cheese Pie 95
Cherry Hand Pies 38
Cherry Mini Pies 38
Cherry Nut Pie 96
Cherry Pie with Mayonnaise 39
Chess Pie 135

278

Index

Chicken Pie 237, 238, 245
Chicken Schmaltz Pie 240
chocolate 34, 64, 65, 70, 73, 75, 86, 98, 117, 118, 132, 140, 172, 173, 174, 176, 177, 179, 180, 181, 182, 185, 186, 188, 189, 190, 194, 214, 215, 216
Chocolate Almond Pie 172
Chocolate Chess Pie 176
chocolate fried pies 214
Chocolate Ice Box Pie 179
Chocolate Italian Meringue Pie 194
Chocolate Meringue Pie 178, 184, 194, 196, 197, 199
Chocolate Peppermint Pie 182
Chocolate Pie 172, 178, 180, 181, 185
Chocolate Pie with Meringue 196
Cinnamon Cream Pie 97
Cocktail Pecan Pie 269
Coconut Cream Layer Pie 99
Coconut Cream Meringue Pie 201
Coconut Cream Pie 203
Coconut Custard Pie 137
Coconut Meringue Pie 136, 200, 201, 202, 203
Coconut Pecan Pie 69
Coconut Pie 136
Coffee Chiffon Pie 98
Company Apple Pie 40
Company's Comin' Pie 264
Cornmeal Pie 137
Cottage Cheese Pie 99
Cran-Raspberry Pie 59
crust 20, 21, 22, 23, 24, 25, 26, 30
Cushaw Pie 138
Custard Pie 220
Daisy's Lunchbox French Amaretto Peach Pie 42
Dang Good Pie 139
David Pryor's Favorite Blueberry Torte 91
DeVito's Restaurant Bourbon Chocolate Pecan Pie 65
Dog Tick Pie 267
Dogwood Hills Brown Sugar Buttermilk Pie 126
Dogwood Hills Cannoli Pie 132

Dora May Pearson's Sweet Potato Pie 163
Dreamsicle Pie 140
Dutch Vanilla Cream Pie 142
Ed and Kay's Chocolate Meringue Pie 199
Ed and Kay's Lemon Meringue Pie 205
Egg Custard Pie 142, 145, 146
Elvis Presley 96
English Apple Pie 41
Evelyn Weldon's Chocolate Almond Pie 172
Evelyn Weldon's Pie Crust 26
Fat Free Pie Crust 25
Fawn Pie 267
Flintrock Strawberry Cream Pie 101
Forgotten Pie 146
Franke's Cafeteria Egg Custard Pie 143, 145
Frappuccino Pie 102
French Amaretto Peach Pie 42
French Apple Pie 42
French Chocolate Pie 182
Fresh Peach Pie 103
Fresh Peach Pie like Bryce's Cafeteria 103
Fresh Pear Tart 44
fried pies 212, 213, 216, 218
Frito Chili Pie 244
Fudge Brownie Pie 221
Fudge Cream Pie 184
Funeral Pie 268
Furr's Cafeteria Millionaire Pie 110
Galaktobourero 269
Gee, You Look Terrific 279
German Chocolate Pecan Pie 70
Girl Scout Lemon-Up Pie 104
gluten-free 24, 126, 132
Gluten-Free All-Butter Pie Crust 24
Gluten-Free Brown Sugar Buttermilk Pie 126
Goodie Pie 222
Gooseberry Handmade Pies Lard Crust 26
Gooseberry Pie 44

Gooseberry's Handmade Pies Chocolate Italian Meringue Pie 194
graham cracker crust 39, 62, 86, 90, 94, 95, 96, 97, 98, 105, 106, 107, 109, 111, 112, 113, 114, 115, 117, 119, 140, 148, 153, 174, 179, 181, 182, 189, 204
Granny's Chocolate Pie 180
Great Googly Moogly 280
Greek Milk Pie 269
Greenhouse Grille's Bourbon Chocolate Chunk Pecan Pie 64
Green Tomato Pie 270
hand pies 215, 217
Hershey Bar Pie 185
Hickory Nut Pie 71
Holiday Sparkle Delight Pie 105
Homemade Single Pie Crust 23
Homemade Vegetable Shortening Pie Crust 24
Honey Sweet Potato Pie 147
Hot Water Pie Crust 22
Huckleberry Pie 212
I'm a big fan of cheese 280
Irma's Sweet Potato Pie 164
Jamie McAfee's Peanut Butter Ice Cream Pie 115
Jamie McAfee's Peppermint Ice Cream Pie 118
Jan's Fresh Peach Pie 53
Japanese Fruit Pie 271
Joy Choy Pie 272
Karo Nut Pie 72
Kat Robinson's Mushroom Pie 248
Kelli Marks's Blueberry Chess Pie 124
Kelli Marks's Sinfully Sweet Sweet Potato Pie 166
Kentucky Derby Pie 73
Key Lime Pie 148
KJ Zumwalt's Apple Pie 30
Kopper Kettle Smokehouse Millionaire Pie 111
lard 26, 48, 60
Layered Vegetable Parmesan Pie 243
lemon 28, 34, 45, 74, 104, 105, 106, 107, 108, 110, 124, 150, 149, 204, 205, 206, 207, 222
Lemon Chess Pie 149, 150
Lemon Cream Cheese Pie 104
Lemon Cream Meringue Pie 204
Lemon Cream Pie 105
Lemon Ice Cream Pie 106
Lemon Improv Pie 107
Lemon Meringue Pie 204, 206, 207
Lemon Pecan Pie 74
Lemon Raspberry Tart 45
Lemon Rice Pie 107
Lemon-Up Pie 104
Lennie's Flintrock Strawberry Cream Pie 101
lime 86
Lindsey's Hospitality House Sweet Potato Pie 164
Lisa Hackett's Peanut Butter Meringue Pie 209
Little Fried Pies 213
Loretta's Peanut Butter Pie 116
Luby's Chocolate Chess Pie 177
Luscious Lemon Pie 108
Makes Its Own Crust Raisin Pie 223
Mama Jo's Flaky Crust 30
Mandarin Orange Pie 109
Mandi's German Chocolate Pecan Pie 70
Maple Cream Pie 151
Mary Thomas's Karo Nut Pie 72
Matthew McClure's Pecan Pie 80
Maude Brannon's Coconut Pie 200
Melinda's No-Bake Cheese Chiffon Pie 112
Mellow Mai Tai Pie 110
meringue 101, 107, 136, 152, 172, 178, 184, 192, 193, 194, 196, 197, 199, 201, 202, 203, 204, 205, 207, 208, 210, 272
Millionaire Pie 110, 111
Mincemeat Pie 244
Miss Betty's Pecan Pie 82

Index

Miss Mary's Lemon Meringue Pie 207
Mockingbird Kitchen's
    Mockingbird Pie 186
Mockingbird Pie 186
Mother McQuay's Orange Pie 151
Mrs. Miller's Chicken Pot Pie 245
Ms. Lena's Squash Pie 161
Muffaletta Pie 247
mushroom 248, 259
Mushroom Pie 248
Mushroom Sour Cream Pie 248
Myrtie Mae's Possum Pie 189
Nana Deane's Coconut Pecan Pie 69
Nellie B's Peach Pie 54
Nutty Chip Pie 75
Oark General Store Pecan Pie 76
Oark General Store's Coconut
    Cream Meringue Pie 201
Oark General Store's Peanut Butter
    Pie 112
Oatmeal Pie 273
Old Faashioned Chocolate Fried
    Pies 214
Old Fashioned Chocolate Hand
    Pies 215
Onion Pie 250
orange 45, 54, 55, 109, 110, 140,
    151, 208, 244
Orange Meringue Pie 208
Orange Pie 151
Oreo Pie 188
Orval Faubus's Favorite Chicken
    Pie 237
Ozark Folk Center Fried Pies 216
Ozark Grape Pie 47

Ozark Wild Huckleberry Pie 48
Paradise Pie 225
Pastrami Pastrami Reuben Pie 251
PattiCakes Kentucky Derby Pie 73
Patty's Pastry Dough 22
PCP Pie 274
peach 53, 54, 56, 92, 103, 113, 152
Peach Custard Pie 152
Peach Pie 54
Peach Vanilla Cream Pie 113
Pea Farm Bistro's Sugar Milk
    Cream Pie 122
Peanut Butter Banana Pie 152
Peanut Butter Cream Pie 114
Peanut Butter Custard Pie 153
Peanut Butter Ice Cream Pie 115
Peanut Butter Meringue Pie 209
Peanut Butter Pie 112, 116, 153,
    209
pear 44, 54, 55
Pear Mincemeat Pie 55
Pear Mincemeat Pie Filling 54
pecan 41, 43, 55, 56, 64, 65, 67, 68,
    69, 70, 72, 73, 74, 75, 76, 77,
    78, 79, 80, 82, 84, 91, 93,
    96, 110, 120, 155, 158, 160,
    163, 166, 170, 176, 182, 186,
    189, 222, 225, 227, 244, 266,
    271, 274
Pecan Coconut Pineapple Pie 274
Pecan Pie 76, 77, 78, 79, 80, 82
Pecan Pies x 10 78
Pecan Tarts 84
peppermint 117, 118, 182
Peppermint Ice Box Pie 117

SHOO-FLY PIE

1 unbaked 9 inch pie shell
1 c. flour
½ c. sugar
4 Tbsp. butter or shortening
½ c. boiling water
½ c. molasses
½ tsp. baking soda
Pinch of cinnamon

Line a deep 9 inch pie plate with pie crust, making a high, fluted rim. In a mixing bowl, combine flour, sugar and butter with your hands until crumbly. In a separate bowl, mix water, molasses, cinnamon and soda. Beat with a spoon until foamy. Pour into pie shell. Add crumb mixture on top of filling and tamp down some of it into the filling, but leave some on top. Bake at 350° for 35 to 40 minutes or until bubbly and brown.

Linnie Jeffries, Retired Health Department

Peppermint Ice Cream Pie 118
Pianalto's Peach Pecan Pie 56
Pickens' Commissary Holiday
    Sparkle Delight Pie 105
pineapple 72, 109, 110, 111, 139,
    155, 222, 244, 266, 267, 274
Pineapple Cream Cheese Pie 155
pinto 154
Pinto Bean Pie 154
Possum Pie 170, 189
Pumpkin Pie 156, 168
Pumpkin Pies x 7 159
Pumpkin Praline Pie 158, 160
Purple Cow Coconut Cream Pie 203
Purple Cow Pecan Pies 78
Purple Cow Pumpkin Pie 159
Rabbit Pie 255, 257
Raisin Pie 268
raspberry 45, 59, 120
Raspberry Cream Cheese Pie 120
Red Hot Apple Pie 57
Rhubarb Cream Pie 210
Rhubarb Pie 58, 59, 210
Rice Pie 226
Ritz Pie 227
Roy Fisher's Cherry Nut Pie 96
Rubert's Rabbit Pie 255
Ruby Jones's Lemon Pecan Pie 74
Ruby Thomas's Paradise Pie 225
Ruby Tuesday Apple Pie 40
Rymolene's Pies Frapuccino Pie 102
Say It Ain't Say's Sweet Potato Pie 165
Say McIntosh's Sweet Potato Pie 165
Seaman's Pie 272
Serious Eats Pastry Crust 20
Shake Shack Peanut Butter Pie 116
Shoney's Strawberry Pie 62
Shoo Fly Pie 281
Sinfully Sweet Sweet Potato Pie 166
So, You Really Like Pie A Lot 1-287
Soy Sweet Potato Pie 161
Snipe Pie 282
Spanikopita 258
Spiced Blackberry Pie 60
Spinach Mushroom Pie 259

Spinach Parmesan Pie 260
Squash Pie 161, 228
Standard Pie Crust 25
strawberry 33, 59, 62, 92, 101
Strawberry Cream Pie 101, 119
Strawberry Pie 62
Sue's Pie Shop Blueberry Cream
    Pie 90
Sue's Pie Shop Cherry Pie 39
Sugar Milk Cream Pie 122
sweet potato 147, 161, 162, 163,
    164, 166, 217
Sweet Potato 165, 166
Sweet Potato Hand Pies 217
Sweet Potato Pie 147, 162, 163,
    164, 165
Sweet South's Key Lime Pie 148
Tamale Pie 260
Tandra Watkins's Brown Sugar Pie 128
Tessie's Chess Pie 135
The Root Cafe's Dreamsicle Pie 140
Toll House Pie 190
tomato 233, 243, 270
Tommye Billing's Caramel Pie 193
Trio's Raspberry Cream Cheese
    Pie 120
True South Pecan Pie 78
Turkey Pot Pie 261
Tusk and Trotter's Arkansas
    Possum Pie 170
Ventris Trail's End Resort's Fresh
    Peach Pie 53
Victorian Sampler's Coconut
    Cream Layer Pie 99
Vinegar Pie 275, 276
Viv Barnhill's Pumpkin Praline Pie 158
Your favorite pie recipe goes on
    page 287
walnut 29, 37, 40, 41, 66, 75, 190,
    223
War Eagle Mill's Peach Custard Pie 152
Williams Tavern Cushaw Pie 138
Wooden Spoon Caramel Pecan
    Cream Cheese Pie 92
Zack Diemer's Cherry Cream
    Cheese Pie 95
Zucchini Pie 262

Index

One more thing I'd like to ask of you, dear reader.

If you have family recipes, whether they're pie recipes or not, I urge you to write them down .Digitize them - even if it's just taking photos of your written recipe - and save them somewhere important. Take photos of the dishes you make.

In the future, when someone else steps up to write about Arkansas food history and goes looking for information, having these resources available will be so very, very valuable.

However, the true treasure you will create is a repository of information about what it is you and your family enjoy consuming, how you break bread together, how you celebrate and what you prefer to eat throughout the year. Eating is the thing we do with all of our senses. Help keep your family memories alive by documenting these humble things. I guarantee, you will be happy you did.

Kat Robinson is Arkansas's food historian and most enthusiastic road warrior. The Little Rock-based author is the producer and Emmy-nominated host of *Arkansas Dairy Bars: Neat Eats and Cool Treats* (2021), the host of the Emmy-nominated documentary *Make Room for Pie: A Delicious Slice of The Natural State* (2018), and host of the Arkansas PBS program *Home Cooking with Kat and Friends*. Robinson is also a member of the Arkansas Food Hall of Fame selection committee, a co-chair of the Arkansas Pie Festival, and the Arkansas fellow to the National Food and Beverage Museum. In 2022, she was selected as Best Author in the *Arkansas Times* Readers Choice Awards.

She has written twelve books on food, most notably *Arkansas Food: The A to Z of Eating in The Natural State*, an alphabetic guide to the dishes, delights and food traditions that define her home state. Two of her more recent travel guides, *101 Things to Eat in Arkansas Before You Die* and *102 More Things to Eat in Arkansas Before You Die* define the state's most iconic and trusted eateries. Robinson's *Another Slice of Arkansas Pie: A Guide to the Best Restaurants, Bakeries, Truck Stops and Food Trucks for Delectable Bites in The Natural State* outlines more than 400 places to find the dessert, an extraordinary accomplishment that took thousands of miles, hundreds of hours and so many bites to properly document and catalogue.

In this book, *The Great Arkansas Pie Book*, Robinson's work comes to a brilliant peak. Amongst the 248 recipes showcased in the tome are heritage restaurants that span decades and even centuries, sourced from restaurants both extant and extinct. There are dozens of pies from church and community cookbooks, samples from still-practicing home cooks, and even a few delights from the writer herself.

Robinson's previous culinary collection, *Arkansas Cookery: Retro Recipes from The Natural State*. In the latter, Robinson examines mid-century cookbooks from all over Arkansas, and delivers more than 100 dishes she researched, redacted, cooked and photographed over the course of just 12 days at The Writers' Colony at Dairy Hollow in Eureka Springs.

There's also the companion book of the same name to the PBS broadcasted documentary *Arkansas Dairy Bars: Neat Eats and Cool Treats*, in which she visited, photographed, and cataloged all 98 dairy bars open in the state at the time of publication, sharing the stories and details of these two-window walk-ups that have thrived even in the toughest times to serve up noshes and nostalgia.

Robinson shares her personal life experiences in *A Bite of Arkansas: A Cookbook of Natural State Delights*, her 2020 culinary memoir, which offers 140 recipes from her years, she both made and photographed. Her dedication to the subject of Arkansas food and search for authentic experiences and flavors to share include creating the very layouts and designs for these books.

Kat Robinson's work has appeared in regional and national publications including *Food Network, Forbes Travel Guide, Serious Eats*, and *AAA Magazines*, among others. Her expertise in food research and Arkansas restaurants has been cited by *Saveur, Eater, USA Today, The Wall Street Journal, The Local Palate, Atlas Obscura, The Outline*, and the Southern Foodways Alliance's *Gravy* podcast, for her knowledge, skills and talents related to food research and documentation.

Her efforts have been celebrated in articles by *Arkansas Good Roads, Arkansas Business, 501 Life Magazine*, the *Northwest Arkansas Democrat-Gazette, Do South*, and the *Arkansas Democrat-Gazette*. She has served as the keynote speaker for numerous festivals, both literary and culinary, and speaks to all sorts of group in an effort, as she says, "to spread the gospel of Arkansas food." While she writes on food and travel subjects throughout the United States, she is best known for her ever-expanding knowledge of Arkansas food history and restaurant culture, all of which she explores on her 1200+ article website, *TieDyeTravels.com*.

Robinson's journeys across Arkansas have earned her the title "road warrior," "traveling pie lady," and probably some minor epithets. Few have spent as much time exploring The Natural State, or researching its cuisine. "The Girl in the Hat" has been sighted in every one of Arkansas's 75 counties, oftentimes sliding behind a menu or peeking into a kitchen.

Kat lives with daughter Hunter and partner Grav Weldon in Little Rock. Contact the author at *kat@tiedyetravels.com* with questions, correspondence, and recommendations.

Books by Kat Robinson

**Arkansas Pie:
A Delicious Slice of the Natural State**
History Press, 2012

**Classic Eateries of the Ozarks
and Arkansas River Valley**
History Press, 2013

Classic Eateries of the Arkansas Delta
History Press, 2014

**Another Slice of Arkansas Pie: A Guide to the
Best Restaurants, Bakeries, Truck Stops and Food
Trucks for Delectable Bites in The Natural State**
Tonti Press, 2018

**Arkansas Food:
The A to Z of Eating in The Natural State**
Tonti Press, 2018

101 Things to Eat in Arkansas Before You Die
Tonti Press, 2019

**102 More Things to Eat in Arkansas
Before You Die**
Tonti Press, 2019

**43 Tables:
An Internet Community Cooks During Quarantine**
Tonti Press, 2020

**A Bite of Arkansas:
A Cookbook of Natural State Delights**
Tonti Press, 2020

Arkansas Dairy Bars: Neat Eats and Cool Treats
Tonti Press, 2021

**Arkansas Cookery:
Retro Recipes from The Natural State**
Tonti Press, 2021

and this book
The Great Arkansas Pie Book
Tonti Press, 2023

More to come soon.

Here are a few pages on which you can write your own pie recipes.

www.ingramcontent.com/pod-product-compliance
Lightning Source LLC
Chambersburg PA
CBHW041125110526
44592CB00020B/2691